MULTILINGUAL MATTERS 122
Series Editor: John Edwards

Beyond Boundaries

Language and Identity in Contemporary Europe

Edited by
Paul Gubbins and Mike Holt

MULTILINGUAL MATTERS LTD
Clevedon • Buffalo • Toronto • Sydney

Library of Congress Cataloging in Publication Data
Beyond Boundaries: Language and Identity in Contemporary Europe
Edited by Paul Gubbins and Mike Holt
Multilingual Matters: 122
Includes bibliographical references and index.
1. Sociolinguistics–Europe. 2. Nationalism–Europe.
I. Gubbins, Paul. II. Holt, Mike. III. Multilingual Matters (Series): 122
P40.45.E85 B49 2002
306.44'094–dc21   2001055814

British Library Cataloguing in Publication Data
A catalogue entry for this book is available from the British Library.

ISBN 1-85359-556-X (hbk)
ISBN 1-85359-555-1 (pbk)

Multilingual Matters Ltd
UK: Frankfurt Lodge, Clevedon Hall, Victoria Road, Clevedon BS21 7HH.
USA: UTP, 2250 Military Road, Tonawanda, NY 14150, USA.
Canada: UTP, 5201 Dufferin Street, North York, Ontario M3H 5T8, Canada.
Australia: Footprint Books, PO Box 418, Church Point, NSW 2103, Australia.

Printed and bound in Great Britain by the Cromwell Press Ltd.

Contents

Introduction

MIKE HOLT and PAUL GUBBINS

The link between language and identity has had a long and varied history; nowhere more so than in Europe. It was in Europe that language became a key element in the emergent nation-states that replaced the old dynasties and empires. In many cases these new nation-states came to share their names with the languages that were so vital for their political legitimacy. This process is still continuing as witnessed in the recent break-up of the multinational USSR, Yugoslavia and Czechoslovakia. In fact it is now the exception that proves the rule; there are only a handful of European states that do not share their name with the dominant language. These include the two states known to all students of bilingualism, Belgium and Switzerland, and of course the United Kingdom. Elsewhere, the reshaping of the map along linguistic and/or ethnic lines marches on. One could add that the new Welsh and Scottish Parliaments are part of this process. In this sense we are still living in an age of nationalisms.

However, this does not mean that we automatically move ever closer to the 'one language, one state' model. There are two good reasons for this; the first concerns the nature of language variation itself and the other the consequences of European colonialism. Briefly, all standard languages share territory with linguistically related nonstandard varieties. Whether these varieties are seen as separate languages, as low-status dialects or as prestige-dialects is not really a linguistic matter but depends on history and politics. Yesterday's dialect may become tomorrow's language claiming political independence for its speakers. As Weinreich famously said, 'a standard language is a dialect with an army and a navy'. One theme running through this volume is that identity is not a mere reflection of reality, a simple form of self-awareness, but rather a socially constructed phenomenon. Identity can change and even the most superficially homogeneous state contains varieties that may form

1

the basis for present or future affiliation. They will, of course, have to fight against the principle of economy of scale and against the vested interests and historical advantages of established standards if they are to gain any political recognition. Furthermore, as variation occurs in all languages, including to a limited extent planned or so-called artificial languages, people may feel the pull of a nonstandard form and not necessarily identify only with the standard. Identity may carry the sense of 'sameness' but it does not have to be unidimensional. Most of the following chapters illustrate this complex and multifaceted nature of language identity.

The other factor working against the monolingual state is the immediate result of mass immigration. Whereas the old European languages were territorially based, this is not the case with newer languages added to the linguistic map since the mid-twentieth century. Migrants from the former colonies of Britain and France, for instance, settled where they could find work, in urban centres close to industry and state-sector employment. Most major European cities now contain a mosaic of ethnic groups speaking languages new to the area. Each language is itself scattered around different cities and is therefore unlikely to be afforded any official territorial recognition, although local government will often support speakers of these languages by providing mother-tongue education, interpreting services and translation of official documents.

Technological advances have also had a profound effect on the maintenance of minority languages. Migrant communities need not be cut off from their homelands in the way many were in the past. Air travel allows swift and affordable physical contact and satellite TV, the internet, telephone, video films and publishing facilitate a range and diversity of linguistic contacts unheard of before. Benedict Anderson argued that the railway and printing press paved the way for the linguistically homogeneous nation-state. The new electronic media offer the possibility of a multilingual nation.

We are not here proposing an explanation based on technological determinism. These media will not by themselves promote and maintain a multilingual society. Without a feeling of language identity and the will to keep a sense of group no amount of digital communication will prevent language shift. Of course, as Edwards (1985) has pointed out, a distinctive group feeling can be maintained without a strong language identity, as is the case in Ireland. But where this identity does exist, the ability to see and hear live news from 'home' is extending the vitality of such languages.

Some voices in Europe are beginning openly to criticise the influence of exogenous languages, which they fear as a threat to national identity. Britain, Germany, Austria, Belgium, and Italy, for example, have all recently seen unrest. These critics see minorities as an external menace without acknowledging how interconnected their histories often are with Europe. European powers not only controlled the economies of their third-world colonies but also exported the notion of linguistic identity as a basis for political legitimacy. Hence in India, when the British-inspired partition plan led to the creation of Pakistan and India, the new states chose to enshrine their political differences in formal recognition of Urdu and Hindi as national languages. So Urdu, for example, came to be an important identity marker partly in contradistinction to English under the Raj and partly as a marker of a Muslim identity in contrast to its neighbour India. In Britain, when the children of Pakistani migrants choose to study a community language, they usually choose Urdu even where their parents speak another language because of its national and religious associations. Urdu, unlike German and French (see this volume), is more widely studied than ever before even though only a minority of Pakistanis speak it.

In fact, where colonialism has had a profound effect on the culture of the colonised, there is often a need to re-establish a separate identity. Caribbean Creole forms have no such religious or national associations but carry important symbolic significance for many black people (see Chapter 10). Speakers do not have to use Creole forms fluently for them still to act as a badge of identity. Furthermore the shared experience of colonisation and Caribbean provenance appears more important than the linguistic differences between various islands, so the younger generation often expresses this commonality by using one Jamaican-based form rather than the Creole of their respective parents. The form of Creole chosen often displays many basilectal features not found in the speech patterns of the older generation.

There are clear similarities between the two very different examples cited above. Firstly, the indigenous languages in both the Indian sub-continent and the Caribbean have been heavily influenced by the colonial experience both structurally and in the way they relate to the state. In fact, in the case of the Caribbean, Creole emerged as a direct result of the suppression of the African languages of plantation workers. Secondly, the language identity chosen by children of migrants is not a simple attachment to the language of their parents but involves choice and change. The choices made by such speakers have different symbolic and affective meanings in a European context to those 'back home'. For a young black man born of Barbadian parents and living in London the choice of a Jamaican patois has a very different social signification from how it would be perceived in Barbados.

Thirdly, post-colonial language identity becomes more complex and multifaceted. Attachment, symbolic or otherwise, to an exogenous language does not preclude identity with local variants of English and/ or Standard English. Identity can therefore be additive and does not necessarily involve the loss of one older form and its replacement by another. Whether this is a temporary phenomenon which is part of a process of language shift or whether it is of a more enduring nature only time will tell.

This is one aspect of the meaning of 'beyond boundaries'. Identity involves not only 'sameness' but by extension 'otherness'. In knowing who we are like we also know who we are not like, and this sense of identity is dependent to some extent on an understanding of boundary, where that with which we identify stops. Hybrid identities clearly go beyond ordinary notions of boundary, as individuals cross some boundaries to join others. The invention of the nation-state had already persuaded people to identify with something in addition to the traditional social structures of family, clan and religion. However, this could be seen as expansion into ever-larger units radiating like concentric circles with the individual at the centre, the family as part of the clan and the clan as part of the nation/ethnic group, etc. Hybrid identities involving plural language affiliation and national allegiance cannot be so envisaged and require individuals to move beyond the circle for them to establish some kind of continuity with the past. If there is no link with the past then individuals feel uprooted and alienated, particularly when they compare themselves with the dominant language culture which will invariably have mythologised its own past. Minority language speakers may also have mythologised their past and they often lack the opportunity to identify completely with the dominant culture because they are perceived as outsiders.

In this sense hybrid identities should be seen for what they are; an attempt to link or acknowledge the past in the light of a different cultural environment rather than a mark of disloyalty. Those with origins outside Europe can hardly be expected to believe exclusively in the grand narrative of the new nation when they already carry with them the narrative of the old. In many ways cultural hybridity is a sign of health, for surely Europe knows only too well the dangers of over-identification with one monolithic high culture. Such over-identification can easily form the basis for hatred of that which is not part of the group and which is therefore ultimately damaging for both the self and for the body politic. Racist, fundamentalist and extreme nationalist ideologies rely on this narrow and exclusive form of identity. According to Hans Saner (1986: 50), the antidote is 'identity distance' where an awareness of multiple identity prevents one from being too close to a given ideology, thereby avoiding the trap of hating others while allowing one to remain a real person. What Saner implies by this is not simply that those individuals with hybrid identities are spared the worst excesses of hatred of others but also that it is in the interests of all to acknowledge that the nation is polyethnic and polyglot. This seems particularly important at the time and place of writing when many of the mill towns around the north-west of England have experienced some of the worst unrest seen for years. The repeated charge that Asian communities have not assimilated quickly enough or sufficiently enough to be integrated into the local community reveal an unwillingness to accept such hybridity despite the evidence that younger generations have different patterns of language use (see Chapter 11).

There is, of course, a more obvious sense in which 'beyond boundaries' refers to contemporary Europe and that is in relation to territorial boundaries. It is precisely because the idea of the nation has remained so strong, despite reports of its imminent demise, that territorial boundaries are being called into question. It is fashionable to talk about the end of the nation-state these days, saying that it is either too small to work efficiently in a globalised economy, or that it is too large to be democratically accountable. The alternatives, according to advocates of this view, are supra-national units like the EU at one end and regional government or city states at the other. But all the border changes seen in Europe over the last few decades, the reunification of Germany, the division of the Soviet Union, Yugoslavia and Czechoslovakia, all point to the continuing partition of political units along ethnocultural lines with language as one of the most important factors in national identity. It is not, of course, the only factor; religion and shared history can exert equally powerful claims.

Why should the nation continue to command such loyalty considering its difficult and often bloody history? According to Michael Lind (2000), it is because 'the ethnic nation is the largest community with which ordinary human beings can have an emotional attachment'. People remain attached to other smaller units such as region or town but not to anything larger than the nation. Identity as sameness seems to require some cultural commonality not readily available with larger supra-national organisations. It is easier for a Milanese to feel Italian while believing in the EU than to feel European but merely believe in Italy.

Over much of Europe there is also a weakening of other traditional ties such as religion and kinship, which have helped place the individual in society, and this has increased the relative importance of other markers such as language, region and nation. In areas where there is a strong sense of cultural commonality which is not shared with the dominant culture of the state there is often a desire for territorial recognition of this identity. Those with the strongest sense of difference commonly call themselves nationalists while the state may label them as separatists. Once created on the principle of a common language, modern states appear to resist attempts to use the same principle to pull them apart. They have a lot invested in their boundaries and do not give them up easily.

What they are more prepared to contemplate is some form of official multilingualism within existing boundaries. When the nation-state was a new idea it was important to maintain unity and boundaries for fear that the old dynasty or *ancien régime* would return; hence Fichte claimed not only a strong link between language and soil but also denigrated other languages. Now that the risk has gone, states can afford to be more accommodating. As Anderson says, 'In a world in which the nation state is the overwhelming norm, all of this means that nations can now be imagined without linguistic commonality' (1983: 123). Many states are now more tolerant of minority languages and the systematic and targeted attempts to eradicate languages such as Welsh, Breton, Occitan and Catalan are thankfully a thing of the past. Whether such tolerance will be shown to exogenous languages is dependent on a number of factors including their own vitality and degree of maintenance, the attitude of the speakers and their political influence.

What is clear from all the contributions in this volume is that language identity in Europe is diverse, complex and ever changing. Some contributions focus on the territorial and regional issues and others on the multiple identities associated with migration and urban environments. Some are concerned with identity in relation to the state and others with the individual's sense of identity. Thus Stephen Barbour, in Chapter 1, adopts a broad approach and examines nationalist and internationalist discourse. The former, Barbour argues, assumes every nation should have its own nation-state in which the national language should dominate; language and national identity are thus allied. Internationalist discourse, however, demonstrates awareness not only of languages spoken by small groups but also of English as a global lingua franca. Nevertheless, much internationalist discourse overstates the dominance of English in international exchanges. With this in mind, Barbour examines policies at national and international level to bring education into line with the need for effective communication across language boundaries.

Jenny Cheshire continues the debate about English and points to shifts in the spoken language which reflect changes in young people's identity. In Chapter 2 Cheshire draws on research on dialect levelling in contrastive English towns. Through variable use of certain vowels and certain nonstandard grammatical features, young people construct both regional and class identity. Cheshire compares the situation with continental Europe where English in daily life means it can have a role in young people's expression – or construction – of their multiple identities. Cheshire suggests young people respond emotionally to English, not only learning it but also incorporating it into youth language. For many, Cheshire continues, English has become separated from association with native speakers in the UK and elsewhere. Although it is reasonable to worry that English could dominate in a multilingual Europe, the present situation augurs well for the development of European identity.

Richard Trim makes a similar point with regard to dominance by a particular language. He asks whether meanings of words in European languages are coming closer together. In Chapter 3 Trim suggests that, despite the continuing internationalisation of lexis in technology, business and politics, the foundations of languages embodied in long-standing concepts of the lexicon are likely to preserve their own semantic identity. This appears particularly to be the case, says Trim, with the figurative lexicon where cross-fertilisation of meaning has not prevented a proportion of the lexicon choosing paths specific to either one language or groups of languages. To illustrate his point Trim analyses the shared metaphor 'dryness' in English and French.

Paul Gubbins maintains the European theme but takes a wider look at language policy and the resulting confused linguistic identity in the European Union. He claims the EU is ill-prepared for the linguistic consequences of enlargement to possibly 25 nations. In Chapter 4 Gubbins looks at the gap between policy and practice in the EU and considers some of the options to bridge it. These include proposals tabled by the Italian *Partito Radicale* to the Committee for Institutional Affairs of the European Parliament involving *inter alia* Latin and Esperanto. Gubbins concludes the EU has a long way to go before reaching consensus on a democratic language policy. However, the fact that the EU is now starting to consider the language issue suggests it may yet avoid the fate envisaged by the Radical Party that the 'lack of a lasting solution for the language problem may threaten long term political cohesion of the European Union'.

A more specific approach is taken by Harald Haarmann, who examines the implications of the feminine gender in determining Russian identity in the post-Soviet era. In Chapter 5 Haarmann highlights the efforts of leaders such as Lenin to play down nationalistic overtones in a concept such as 'Mother Russia'. Nevertheless the linguistic pull of feminism as a form of national identity proved so strong that even in the 1960s it was reflected, despite prevailing communist doctrine, in national monuments. Haarmann concludes that as a result of the current stalemate between the conflicting ideologies of moderates and reformers – as well as incursions into the Russian language by English – there is a yearning in Russia (but not in former Soviet states) for the historical security of the past epitomised by 'Mother Russia'. Nevertheless, as Haarmann demonstrates, there are dangers for modern-day Russians in clinging too closely to their past.

A similar crisis of language, politics and identity is helping reshape other regions of Europe. In Chapter 6 Brendan Murphy, Cristina Diaz-Varela and Salvatore Coluccello draw a distinction between regional policies in Spain and Italy. They note that Catalonia has a coherent national identity born of centuries of distinct development from the Spanish state whereas Padania is more a political construct than a social reality. Here, achievements of the separatists remain disparate and elusive; in comparison with Catalonia there is little to show for separatist ambitions. Nevertheless both Padania and Catalonia, the most prosperous regions of Italy and Spain, continue to press for increased autonomy and even secession. The authors analyse the contributions of both areas to the construction of separate regional identities in their respective countries.

Sue Wright adopts a historical perspective to illuminate identity changes facing border regions. Wright considers that many of these regions are spearheading cross-frontier initiatives in the context of a Europe of the regions. She illustrates the point in Chapter 7 and looks at relations between Nice and the Italian world, in particular between 1855–1865. She suggests that the realignment from the House of Savoy to incorporation in the French state was so swift and so complete that it cut Nice from its old links and networks. Rapid adoption of French, for instance, in administration and public life, and the same process of shifting identity, can be seen to some extent in present-day Europe through 'colonisation' by English.

Mike Holt remains with French as a 'colonising' language but brings the debate firmly into the present. He looks at the increasingly violent conflict between the proponents of French and Arabic for the right to represent Algerian identity. In Chapter 8 Holt argues that although Algeria is often portrayed as a country assimilated into French culture and language, this was never truly the case. Universalist claims for French, says Holt, provide strong cultural identity but also contain a weakness. The same universalist claims enabled Algeria after independence to seek another universalism, one associated not with French language and culture but with Arab nationalism. Nevertheless, while education has been Arabised, the path to personal advancement in Algeria is still French. Accordingly Arab and Berber Algerian writers regard French as 'booty' captured in war to be used against the coloniser. Islamists now claim a greater universalism for Arabic yet, as Holt indicates, one state cannot accommodate two universalisms, neither of which contains specific Algerian identity.

Michael Anderson moves the debate about identity from a wider, international level to a narrower, domestic one. He assumes that marriages between individuals of different nationalities in Europe give rise to theoretical and practical questions of child identity and child-raising; these might include how children in bicultural families are socialised to 'belong' and how culturally differentiated parental roles affect a child's activities and development. In Chapter 9 Anderson takes a social anthropological perspective and offers an insight into cultural 'boundaries' in domestic family settings. Drawing on fieldwork from Greek/British households Anderson notes that the child can sometimes be a co-creator of its own partisan or hybrid identity rather than a receptacle of parental beliefs. He substantiates his arguments via children's use of language in the home and beyond.

Lerleen Willis undertakes a similar study but moves the investigation nearer home. She draws on empirical work examining Creole-English bilingualism. In Chapter 10 Willis highlights the manner in which second- and third-generation African-Caribbeans in Britain overcome the constraints of societal attitudes and prejudice. For these people, says Willis, the fact that their mother tongue or language of the home is often a Creole, a low-status language, complicates recognition of bilingual competence. Nevertheless these young people are able to define a personal and group identity based on in-group language. The author notes that for many young African-Caribbeans in Britain there is a reluctance to embrace the culture and identity of the land into which they were born. Accordingly Creole maintenance among the sample population supports the desire to maintain a separate black (African) identity in a wider British and, by analogy, European context.

Mike Reynolds, in another study centred on Sheffield, offers a different perspective on minority language use in Britain. Reynolds' focus is mixed code. In Chapter 11 he reports on a three-year study into Punjabi/Urdu by bilingual speakers which hypothesised linkage between social network membership, code-switching behaviours and language maintenance/shift. He shows that gradual language shift is taking place and suggests why the process is slow. Reynolds highlights two features: the relationship between the community languages involved – Punjabi and Urdu – and evidence for existence of a mixed code. The Punjabi-Urdu situation is classically diglossic which has led to a policy among parents (in three of the families in the study) of speaking only Urdu to their children. Reynolds illustrates and discusses this policy. At the same time he sees development of 'mixed code' in Sheffield as an example of widespread language contact found among ethnic minority communities.

The contributions in this volume therefore present a kaleidoscope of shifting identities and loyalties in Western Europe and beyond. To those born and bred into the relative stability of white middle-class Britain it might appear that much of the discussion in this book is distant and irrelevant. Not so. As depicted here, in chapter after chapter, change – whether at transnational, national, regional or local level – is manifest in a variety of linguistic and other ways. The change is gradual, and perhaps not immediately apparent – but we ignore it at our peril. To refuse to move beyond present borders, to fail to acknowledge their fluidity, is to atrophy, to deny existence itself; above all it is to ignore the lessons of the past and present and to fail to apply them to the future.

References

Anderson, B. (1983) *Imagined Communities: Reflections on the Origins and Spread of Nationalism.* London: Verso.
Edwards, J. (1985) *Language, Society and Identity.* London: Blackwell.
Lind, M. (2000) National Good. *Prospect.* October.
Saner, H. (1986) Von den Gefahren der Identität für das Menschein. In Benedetti, Gaetano and Wiseman (eds) *Ein Inuk sein: Interdisziplinäre Vorlesungen zun Problem der Identität.* Göttingen.

Chapter 1

Language, Nationalism and Globalism: Educational Consequences of Changing Patterns of Language Use

STEPHEN BARBOUR

The following views stem in particular from the book *Language and Nationalism in Europe*, edited jointly with Cathie Carmichael (Barbour and Carmichael, 2000), in which the editors and the other contributors[1] examine the interrelations between language and nationalism in the various states of Europe. The book starts, in a sense, from a nationalist perspective, not because we are nationalists, but because this perspective forms a useful point of departure. A nationalist perspective tends to assume that every individual can be unambiguously classified as belonging to a particular nation, that every nation has a relatively easily definable territory, and that every nation could, in its territory, constitute a sovereign independent nation-state, although not all do at any given time. Frequently in Europe, though very much less frequently elsewhere, the nationalist perspective assumes that each nation has a clearly distinct national language, peculiar to that nation. I hardly need to say that this perspective is based to a great extent on illusion. We found it a useful starting point, however, since it enabled us to highlight the political problems which arise in the many cases where such nationalist discourse clashes with reality.

To make my own position clear, I regard nationalism as highly problematic, since its inherent classification and division of human beings harbours great potential for injustice and conflict.[2] The book, and this chapter, focus on Europe not because we are intentionally eurocentric in our perspective but simply because it is particularly in Europe that language is so closely bound up with nationalism.

The data that we accumulated on the highly varied interrelations between language and nationalism will, I hope, prove useful for stimulating further research; we have so far been able to describe more or less how academics, politicians and journalists see the place of language in the self-image of the various nations, and we now need to investigate to what extent other sections in society share their vision. There is great scope for further research, and this chapter is intended more as a signpost to future research than as a report on work completed.

Many politicians and journalists adopt a generally nationalistic public discourse, not necessarily because this reflects their personal beliefs but perhaps more because they believe this is what the public wants to hear. Furthermore, with respect to language, most states operate generally nationalistic language policies, but with enormous variation across the continent. An important outcome of such policies is the weakening of minority languages. This can arise from many types of action, ranging from the physical removal of their speakers (for example in the many episodes of ethnic cleansing in European history) to benign neglect, as in the case of Channel-Islands French. Something highlighted by our research is the importance of the attitudes of the speakers of the minority language themselves, which range from the great insistence on using the language found among speakers of Catalan, to the sentimental attachment to Irish in Ireland which is often not matched by a desire to speak it. Striking is the frequency with which the very conceptualisation of a particular language may relate to the strength of national feeling in the group in question. Speakers of Catalan, although it is linguistically close to Castilian, have a clear conception of a distinct Catalan language while speakers of Breton, utterly distinct from French, identify much more strongly with local dialects than with a Breton language, in the absence of strong Breton nationalism (Mari Jones, personal communication). There is great scope here for further research into the highly varying levels of language loyalty not only among minorities but also among speakers of majority languages

Another deleterious effect of nationalistic policies on language use is monolingualism. Monolingualism means the ability to operate effectively only in one language. It represents a considerable handicap but probably only affects a minority of the world's population, chiefly in Europe and the Americas. In contrast, bilinguals and multilinguals operate effectively in more than one language and, moreover, may find it a great deal easier to acquire further languages; however, in both monolinguals and multilinguals there is great individual variation in language-learning proficiency. Monolingualism arises chiefly in centralised nation-states whose promotion of the national language leads them to prevent those most readily able to learn languages – young children – from being exposed to any language other than the national one. Exposure to other languages will then be too little and too late. In such states there can even arise the quite counter-factual belief that multilingualism is abnormal and problematic (for some more refined argument on the issues, see Edwards, 1994: 55–88).

Language and Globalism

Nationalism is an important motivator for many groups and individuals but also important, alongside self-interest or the interests of kin and neighbours, is globalism. Many people are motivated at least some of the time by the interests of the species or even the planet. Although I use here 'international' and 'global' and their derivatives interchangeably, I would prefer to use 'global' and its derivatives throughout, since 'international' implies that people can act only on a global level through the intermediary of the nation, which need not be so. I have, however, felt obliged to avoid some (potential) derivatives of 'global', such as 'globalist', which are not current English usage.

A global perspective recognises the need for an international language. The response to this need on the part of many internationalists is to use English, a most important point considered below. A global perspective poses little real threat to national languages or indeed minority languages; globalism seems able to co-exist with linguistic and cultural pluralism. The international language, be it English or the earlier international language French (which still to an extent retains this role), tends to influence other languages, but not generally replace them in all spheres of life. While internationalists may switch to an international language for aspects of work, they show little sign of doing so for leisure activities and in the family. In contrast, while nationalists often succeeded in persuading speakers of minority languages that their language represented backwardness or disloyalty, no similar campaigns are mounted on behalf of international languages. The reasons for this differing progress of national and international languages are fascinating and profound (see Edwards, 1985).

The consequences of espousing both internationalist and nationalist perspectives can impinge on many aspects of personal and professional life, for instance the professional activity in which many academics are engaged, namely language teaching.

There is a widespread perception of crisis in the teaching of languages other than English in Britain. This can be summed up in the statement:

'There are too few students taking languages beyond a very elementary level' (see Boaks, 1998). Many reasons for this are suggested. As a teacher of German I often hear the argument: 'We have too few students of German because of the entrenched position of French'. This misses the point; there are too few students of every other language simply because of the position of English. I am astonished how rarely this argument is put (it is not prominent, for example, in Moys, 1998) because, in my view, it is patently obvious. One reason this argument is not debated is that, at least in our capacity as language teachers, we sometimes engage in a nationalist discourse. We speak as if English was 'our' language, and bemoan the fact that 'they' can all speak our language, but we cannot speak their languages. We also convey the impression that other countries are, like Britain, publicly monolingual;[3] we tend to imply, for example, that to function in Germany you have to know German. Sadly this often fails to convince students, since the Germans they meet (incidentally not a social cross-section – a point further discussed below) can often communicate reasonably well in English.

We may then try to tell students they require other languages for the sound educational reason that they need to understand other cultures. This may also be unconvincing. Many students know they can encounter cultural variety in all major cities through the medium of English; they might also notice that for instance Paris or Frankfurt are also multicultural and that cultural differences between some European groups, such as (traditionally) Protestant North Germans and (traditionally) Protestant white English people are not great. In other words we imply a close one-to-one relationship between languages, cultures, nations and states which is, quite simply, counterfactual. Incidentally, if we were really serious about languages for multicultural education we might be teaching Yoruba, Arabic or Punjabi.

If English is the global language, why are other languages needed? Firstly, educational reasons. While learning other languages may not be a prerequisite for encountering other cultures, it is often indispensable to a deep and detailed understanding of such cultures. Those who find at any stage of their lives that they wish to engage in such study are likely to find the language learning required much more difficult if they are strictly monolingual.

Languages are also important for understanding other societies, as distinct from other cultures. German, for example, while not clearly providing an insight into sharply different cultures, does enable us, if we study it to an adequate level, to gain knowledge of a different society. In German society the various social, ethnic and cultural groups may or may not resemble social, cultural and ethnic groups found in Britain (though some are strikingly similar), but what is different is the relationship between them. For example, class differences in the white indigenous German ethnic group are less significant than differences in the parallel group in Britain; education has a different place in society; political and economic systems are significantly different; minority ethnic groups are even more marginalised than they are in Britain, and so on.

Perhaps the most important educational reason for teaching other languages is to free students from the prison of monolingualism. If we take this seriously, then we have to make much more effort to introduce other languages to children at an earlier age. Attempts to do this so far have met with only limited success, for various avoidable reasons (see Boaks, 1998); the effort must be made again.

There are also utilitarian reasons for learning other languages. The view of English as the global language is over-stated. If we look just at the German language and Germany, it is indeed true that many German-speakers can communicate in English. Those who can, however, are more likely to be educated, younger westerners. To communicate with anyone who does not fulfil these criteria it is helpful to know German. It is also interesting to note that, partly for ideological reasons, younger, liberal Germans may over-state the global significance of English. I have personally witnessed Germans giving themselves unnecessary problems by trying to use English in Greece where, because of the large numbers of former 'guest workers' who have returned to Greece from Germany, in some circumstances German is better understood than English.

There are also functional reasons for learning other languages for business purposes. The reasons have been well rehearsed, for example by Nigel Reeves and others (see Liston and Reeves, 1985): the need to have a thorough understanding of the culture and society of the group in question; the public-relations value of meeting customers half way; the usefulness of being able to understand what partners or competitors are saying when they talk among themselves.

One of the most important instrumental reasons for speakers of English to learn other languages is to provide high-quality translators. It is axiomatic among many translators that the highest quality of translation is most likely to be achieved by those translating into their language of habitual use. It would be possible to rest the argument there but, if I did so, I would expose myself to challenge. Two of the arguments that could be used against me I will now outline and attempt to rebut.

The Challenge

On a practical level it could be objected that we will never have enough fluent English-speakers who can translate out of the languages that are hardly taught in English-speaking countries. This is a valid point, but it can nevertheless be argued that, with modern communications, it is not unrealistic to attempt to provide a speaker of any language with a course in any other language; it is possible to go at least some way towards meeting this challenge.

The second argument is more complex. It could be argued there is no problem in relying for translators on speakers of every other language who have learnt English. This argument actually arises from premises accepted in sociolinguistics and must be taken seriously. It runs thus:

- Every language can potentially express any concept, every language is an equally valid system of communication.
- Every social or geographical variety, any dialect of any language, can potentially express any concept. This includes L2 varieties, varieties used by those for whom English is clearly not a first language.
- If therefore L2 varieties depart from standard English, as used by those who speak English as a first language, there can be no possible objection. They are valid varieties of English, with which – for instance – the middle-class white speaker of English born in England simply has to come to terms.

Nevertheless, coming to terms with such varieties of English can be problematic. It is encountered, for example, in certain academic journals published either wholly or partly in English but which are either edited in Germany (such as *Sociolinguistica*) or edited in Britain by non-linguists (such as *German Politics*). In such journals many German-speakers simply write in English, and this then seems not to be edited for English expression, resulting in frequent minor, sometimes major comprehension difficulties. The problem is most acute in humanities and social sciences; in the natural sciences much of the communication is in the form of mathematical expressions which are truly a uniform, global means of communication. Part of the problem, it can be assumed, arises from lack of linguistic awareness on the part of the authors. They may imagine that because they function well in spoken English, where reliance can also be placed on non-linguistic signals or where they can immediately seek explanation or clarification, that their use of the written language is equally efficient.

A different view of the problem could, however, come from socio-linguists concerned with Creole languages. I would not wish to push this argument too far since there are many important differences, but it is worth remembering that L2 varieties of English may, like Creole languages, exhibit strong substratum influence from other languages. Creole languages can be classified as languages distinct from English, from and into which translation takes place. The varieties of English used by L2 speakers could be treated similarly; as entirely valid means of communication but as perhaps inappropriate for written communication, in certain registers at least, with an audience of L1 speakers or speakers of other L2 varieties. To assist L2 users of English with certain types of written English communication, we need to train considerable numbers of translators and editors who do not need, incidentally, to be L1 speakers of English but who do need intensive exposure to L1 varieties.

The discipline of translation studies has relatively clear views on these matters. Varieties of English with strong substratum influence may be appropriate in translations of creative writing but translations of academic writing are generally expected to adhere to the norms of standard English used by speakers of English as a first language (for detail on issues involved in training translators see Hatim and Mason, 1997). English-speakers, particularly sociolinguists, tend to look with distaste on the normative activities of the French Academy and the *office de la langue française* (indeed, this distaste can in itself be part of a nationalistic English discourse), but there is perhaps something to be said for some regulation; it is unworkable and undesirable in spoken language, an unacceptable infringement of the right to free expression if legally enforced, but it might help communication in academic writing (for the French situation see Judge, 1993).

One intention of this chapter is to point to future research. Two topics which deserve further work are:

(1) The varying currency of English as an international language; there are beginnings (for example in McArthur, 1996) but much more detail is required particularly, for example, in eastern and southern Europe. In both these areas it seems possible that German plays a larger role than is publicly recognised.
(2) The characteristics of the usage of English as a second language, particularly in the social sciences and in business communication; are there really communication problems in this field?

In conclusion, it can be said that it is possible to adopt nationalist and internationalist discourses about language use. When faced with the crisis in language teaching, those involved in the profession may adopt a nationalist discourse even if, as is frequently the case, they adopt internationalist positions on other issues. Teachers are unconvincing in this and have to accept the internationalist argument, whether they like it or not, that English is, or is becoming, a global language.

Teachers also have to adopt varied arguments to defend the teaching of languages other than English: knowledge of more than one language provides general educational benefit and offers escape from mono-lingualism; although not indispensable, it can bring benefit in business; it satisfies the pressing need – which will not diminish – for people who can cross language boundaries, for interpreters of languages and of cultures. English may be an international language but it is not yet, and never will be, the only language.

Notes
1. Other contributors are Anne Judge, Clare Mar-Molinero, Lars Vikør, Robert Howell, Carlo Ruzza, Barbara Tørnquist-Plewa and Peter Trudgill.
2. There is copious literature on nationalism. Somewhat contrasting views are presented in Anderson (1983), Smith (1983) and Hobsbawm (1990).
3. Britain is not really monolingual, and never has been, but this is how it is perceived, at least by a majority.

References
Anderson, B. (1983) *Imagined Communities*. New York: Verso.
Barbour, S. and Carmichael, C. (eds) (2000) *Language and Nationalism in Europe*. Oxford: Oxford University Press.
Boaks, P. (1998) Languages in schools. In A. Moys (ed.) *Where Are We Going with Languages?* London: Nuffield Foundation.
Edwards, J. (1985) *Language, Society and Identity*. Oxford: Blackwell.
Edwards, J. (1994) *Multilingualism*. London: Routledge.
Hatim, B. and Mason, I. (1997) *The Translator as Communicator*. London: Routledge.
Hobsbawm, E.J. (1990) *Nations and Nationalism since 1780*. Cambridge: Cambridge University Press.
Judge, A. (1993) French: A planned language? In C. Sanders (ed.) *French Today. Language in its Social Context* (pp. 7–26). Cambridge: Cambridge University Press.
Liston, D. and Reeves, N. (1985) *Business Studies, Languages & Overseas Trade*. Plymouth and London: Macdonald & Evans and the Institute of Export.
McArthur, T. (1996) English in the world and in Europe. In R. Hartmann (ed.) *The English Language in Europe* (pp. 3–15). Oxford: Intellect.
Moys, A. (ed.) (1998) *Where Are We Going with Languages?* London: Nuffield Foundation.
Smith, A.D. (1983) *Theories of Nationalism*. New York: Holmes and Meyer.

Chapter 2

Who We Are and Where We're Going: Language and Identities in the New Europe

JENNY CHESHIRE

The way we use our language reveals our sense of 'who we are' – our personal and social identities. We are many things, though; we have multiple identities, so our language can be expected to be variable to allow us to construct these different aspects of our identities as we speak. Furthermore, since language is intricately related to the social, political and cultural contexts in which we live, analysing current processes of continuity and change in language behaviour can provide us with insights into trajectories of continuity and change in social life generally. My focus here will be the language of young people, since older people are more likely to have reached 'where they are going' in life. In particular, my focus is on the English of young people; first on the English of monolingual speakers in England, and then on the English used by bilingual or multilingual speakers of English in continental Europe.

The Dialect-levelling Project

Some of the language changes currently taking place in urban centres in England can be seen from the results of the dialect-levelling project (Cheshire, Kerswill and Williams, 1999). This project, funded by the UK Economic and Social Research Council, analysed the speech of 96 adolescents aged 14–15 in three towns. Two, Milton Keynes and Reading, are in south-east England, and one, Hull, is in the north-east.

Milton Keynes is Britain's fastest-growing new town. It was founded in 1967 and since then its population has more than quadrupled. Reading

19

is an older, prosperous, established town approximately the same distance from London as Milton Keynes. It has considerable in-migration but, unlike Milton Keynes, it also has a stable local population. In contrast, in Hull there is more out-migration than in-migration, unemployment is high and levels of educational achievement in local schools are low.

Eight boys and eight girls were recorded in two schools in each of the three towns, in two contrasting areas corresponding roughly to 'working-class' and 'middle-class' areas. The recordings were of one-to-one 'ethnographic' interviews, mainly with Ann Williams and occasionally with Paul Kerswill. The young people were also recorded in pairs, in more spontaneous interactions with the fieldworker, as well as in group discussions between four to six speakers, guided by the fieldworker. For comparison, four working-class elderly speakers (aged 70 or over) were also recorded in each town. All the findings reported here are based on this fieldwork. Fuller details of the project are given in Cheshire (1999) Cheshire, Kerswill and Williams (1999), and Williams and Kerswill (1999).

Williams and Kerswill (1999) present complex patterns of continuity and change in some of the phonological features they analysed. Their study of the PRICE vowel provides a good illustration of much of what follows. In the new town of Milton Keynes, where the young people's families came from outside the area and do not, on the whole, have local ties, there is only a small overlap in the realisations of this vowel by the 16 working-class adolescents and the four elderly speakers (these elderly speakers were from Bletchley, the nearest town that pre-existed Milton Keynes). In Reading, on the other hand, where many of the young people are in close contact with older family members from the local area, there *is* continuity in the realisation of this vowel between the elderly speakers and the working-class adolescents. Continuity is not absolute; the young people use the back and centralised variants of the vowel less frequently than the older speakers, but nevertheless there is overlap in the vowel realisations, and the predominant variant for all the working-class speakers is a back, diphthongal [ɑɪ]. In Reading, then, the working-class adolescents reveal their allegiance to the locality through the realisation of this vowel. In Hull the strength of local norms can be seen more strongly still; here the PRICE vowel preserves a complex allophonic patterning, with an [ai] diphthong before voiceless consonants (as in *bright* or *pipe*), and an [aː] monophthong before voiced consonants (as in *bride* or *five*). Thus the realisation of this vowel can be seen to signal the strength of the young people's local or regional identity in the three towns studied.

The strength of local linguistic norms in Hull can also be seen in the distribution of H in lexical words such as *house* or *hand*. In all three towns H-dropping is a feature of the traditional dialects and, as would be expected, the elderly speakers use initial [h] relatively rarely. In Reading and Milton Keynes, however, there is a surprisingly high use of initial [h] amongst the working-class adolescents (Williams and Kerswill, 1999: 158). This is not the case in Hull, however, where the frequency of occurrence of initial [h] was similar for both the adolescents and the elderly speakers. Williams and Kerswill suggest this is because the young working-class Hull speakers, who were living in a close-knit, territorially bounded estate, see the pronunciation of initial [h] as southern and 'posh', and strive to avoid it (1999: 157–8). The connotations of [h] pronunciation are not the same for the young people in the southern towns of Milton Keynes and Reading, and their use of [h] varies accordingly.

It is all the more interesting, therefore, to find that in all three towns the adolescents have adopted some consonant pronunciations which are currently spreading rapidly through England, and that are assumed to originate in London and south-eastern England. These pronunciations are TH-fronting, or the merger of [Θ] with [f] (in, for example, *thing*); the merger of [ð] and [v] in words such as *brother*; and T-glottaling – the use of a glottal stop rather than [t] – in intervocalic position (as in *letter*) and in final position (as in *cut it out*). The elderly speakers do not use these features, but they *are* used by adolescents in all three towns, including Hull, both by the middle-class groups and the working-class groups – though more frequently by the young working-class speakers. Despite their allegiance to local norms of pronunciation, then, young Hull speakers are adopting these new features just as fully as young people in Milton Keynes and Reading.

The explanation appears to lie, at least in part, in affective factors (see Williams and Kerswill, 1999: 162). In all three towns the young people's linguistic identity was formed, in part, in opposition to the idea of 'being posh'. Even the middle-class speakers whose speech would be considered by the working-class group to be 'posh' formed their linguistic identity in opposition to a group whom they in turn considered 'posh' – the 'kids from the private schools, who sound as if they've had elocution lessons' (Kerswill and Williams, 1997). Importantly, for the Hull adolescents, 'posh' speech was London speech. This is a widespread view in northern areas of England. For example, in a previous study of language attitudes (Cheshire and Edwards, 1991) it was found that young people in Widnes, in the north-west of England, associated 'talking posh' with the south of England, particularly London. The youngsters commented, for example, 'I dislike London accent. It sounds really posh' and 'I dislike London accent because they are stuck up snobs' (1991: 232).

Although sociolinguists stress that Received Pronunciation is a social accent, not tied to any region of Britain, for young people in the north of England there seems no doubt that it is associated with London. This presumably accounts for the Hull adolescents' avoidance of initial [h]. The innovating consonant features, on the other hand, which they have apparently been very happy to adopt, are also southern in origin, but are associated, we assume, with nonstandard south-eastern varieties of English rather than with RP (Foulkes and Docherty, 1999: 11). They may also be associated with a general youth culture which is not tied to a particular region. The increase in the number of TV and radio stations and programmes directed at young people has led to widespread use of informal and nonstandard registers in the broadcast media, many of which emanate from London and the south (Williams and Kerswill, 1999: 162). This too can be seen as an affective factor in the spread of features such as these. The result, in any event, is that the adolescents who took part in our research can reveal different aspects of their social identities through their pronunciation of English. These identities include allegiance to the local region, for the Reading and Hull adolescents, a class-based identity, and an identity with an overarching youth culture.

The expression of multiple identities is not limited to the adolescents' pronunciation of English. There are parallels in their morphosyntactic, syntactic and discourse features. For example, in the speech of the working-class adolescents in Reading and Hull, we find localised morphosyntactic features which also occur in the speech of the elderly. In Reading, nonstandard verbal -s and the related nonstandard *has* and *does* are used (e.g. *I wants to be a hairdresser; and you has to wear your blazer in the summer; they does a lot of knitting*). In Hull the zero article occurs (e.g. *there was this fellow beating this other fellow up near flats*) as well as a range of features that do not occur in the southern towns. These include right dislocation (e.g. *he's got a real nice chest him*), a distinctive negative BE paradigm, with [ɪn?] *as the third singular present tense form (she ɪn? going out,* 'she isn't going out') and [a:] *elsewhere in the present (we [a:] going out);* and [wɒn?] as the preterite form for all persons. In addition, negative concord in Hull is organised differently from negative concord in the two southern towns. Negative forms never occur in tags such as *or anything*, in *they don't know what they're doing or anything*, whereas in Reading and Milton Keynes *nothing* and *anything* can both occur in tags of this kind. A number of distinctive lexical forms are used by the Hull adolescents, too, including *twatted* (e.g. *when I'm naughty I get twatted*) and *nowt*, 'nothing' and *owt*, 'anything'. For working-class speakers, there is some continuity with older speakers in the morphosyntax and the vocabulary, just as there is with the realisation of some phonological features; through their use of these features young speakers can show their sense of belonging to their part of the country.

In addition to the localised morphosyntactic and syntactic features, the working-class adolescents in all three towns used some of the nonstandard features thought to be widespread in the urban centres of present-day Britain (Cheshire, Edwards and Whittle, 1989). These include those shown in Figure 2.1: negative concord (e.g. *I like England … I'm happy with it … we haven't got no diseases no nothing*), nonstandard *was* (e.g. *we just held the brake back and we was upside down all the way*), nonstandard *don't* (e.g. *she don't go out much during the week*), the preterite forms *come* and *done* (e.g. *What's your favourite food? – It used to be steak until the mad cow come about*; and *last night we done a bit of larking around*) and nonstandard *them* (e.g. *it's a bit scary when you're walking past all them druggies*). Each of these features awaits further, more detailed analysis but, as Figure 2.1 shows, these widespread forms are used more frequently by the working-class adolescents than the localised forms in Reading (verbal *-s*, nonstandard *has* and *does*) and Hull (the zero article). The middle-class adolescents use these features only sporadically. Thus the young people also express their social class identities through their use of certain common core nonstandard grammatical features. As expected, there are no local grammatical features in the speech of the young people in the new town of Milton Keynes. However, the working-class adolescents' use of the common core nonstandard features, and the division along class lines, is as clear here as it is in the older, established towns.

It is worth noting that this polarisation along class lines is occurring at a time when government educational policy in England and Wales is attempting to construct a uniform national linguistic identity by insisting, through the National Curriculum for English, on the use of standard English in both formal and informal styles of speech in schools. Research suggests a trajectory whereby uniformity will indeed develop, but where there will be two kinds of uniformity in grammar split along social class lines.

Our analysis of the new focus marker *like* (as in *and we were like rushing home and she was like shouting at me*) shows a parallel distribution to the consonant features that express allegiance to a generalised youth culture. This time, however, the origins of the new feature are thought

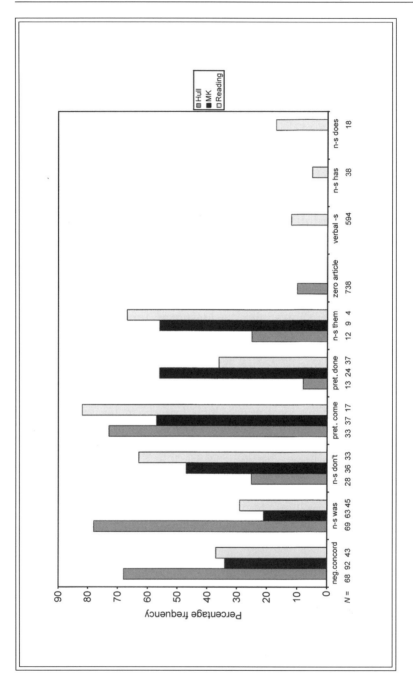

Figure 2.1 Percentage frequencies of nonstandard grammatical features

Table 2.1 Frequency of *like* as focus marker

Group	Number of speakers analysed	Number of words	Number of like	Number of words for one token of like
Hull w.cl. girls	8	16,214	175	92.6
Hull w.cl. boys	8	17,199	179	96.1
Total Hull w.cl.	**16**	**33,413**	**354**	**94.4**
Hull m.cl. girls	4	23,600	412	57.3
Hull m.cl. boys	8	19,302	264	73.1
Total Hull m.cl.	**12**	**42,902**	**676**	**63.5**
MK w.cl. girls	4	11,447	92	124.4
MK w.cl. boys	0			
Total MK w.cl.	**4**	**11,447**	**92**	**124.4**
MK m.cl. girls	8	24,045	245	98.1
MK m.cl. boys	8	27,875	166	167.9
Total MK m.cl.	**16**	**51,920**	**411**	**126.3**
Rdg w.cl. girls	8	15,012	98	153.2
Rdg w.cl. boys	8	14,274	135	105.7
Total Rdg w.cl.	**16**	**29,286**	**233**	**125.7**
Rdg m.cl. girls	4	14,675	88	166.8
Rdg m.cl. boys	2	4,379	31	141.3
Total Rdg m.cl.	**6**	**19,054**	**119**	**160.1**

to be in southern Californian 'valley speak' rather than in the south-east of England (Dailey O'Cain, 2000). Focus *like* and the related marker of reported speech and thought seem rapidly to be innovating globally in urban centres throughout the English-speaking world (Tagliamonte and Hudson, 1999). Our analysis of this feature is not yet completed, but Table 2.1 gives an indication of its use by the adolescents in the three towns. The table suggests that focus marker *like* is widespread among both the working-class and middle-class groups in all three towns. An idea of the rapid spread of this feature can be obtained by comparing its frequency of occurrence in the speech of young working-class speakers in the Reading data (where there is one token of *like* every 125.7 words) with its use by young working-class speakers of the same age in an earlier Reading study (Cheshire, 1982). In the speech of one group of boys in the earlier study (the 'Orts Road' group) there was only one token of *like* in 8948 words. Certainly a more refined analysis is needed for this feature, but it is nevertheless interesting to note that it is used more frequently in Hull than in the other two towns, occurring once per 94.4 words in the working-class group and once per 63.5 words in the speech of the middle-class group. Again, the Hull adolescents can be seen to adopt this new feature just as enthusiastically as the adolescents in Reading and Milton Keynes. Despite their relative isolation, and the strength of their allegiance to local norms, belonging to international youth culture seems to be an important part of their social, and therefore linguistic, identity.

A 'Youth Language'?

The extent of participation in global youth culture by young people who took part in our research can be investigated through their use of features such as *like* and the consonant pronunciations mentioned above. In the interviews there is evidence of a well-defined adolescent culture which is manifested in the magazines the young people read, in the music they listen to, in their clothes and hairstyles, and in their leisure activities. This culture is global, not limited to the English-speaking world, though it is heavily influenced by it. It seems to be affecting languages other than English, giving rise to what some writers have identified as 'youth language' (see, for example, Androutsopoulos, in press). For example, Sankoff *et al.* (1997) document a new use of French *comme*, 'like', in ways that parallel the new uses of *like* as a focus marker and a marker of reported speech and thought in English. Example 1 illustrates both these functions of *comme*.

Example 1
Ah oui on était comme un des seuls, on était peut-être cinq dans mon année qui parlaient les deux langues, puis c'était comme 'wow!' tu sais (oh yeah we were like the only ones, there were about five of us in my year that spoke both languages so it was like 'wow!' you know) (Sankoff *et al.*, 1997).

Example 2 shows a similarly new use of Swedish *ba* to introduce reported speech, and Example 3 shows German *so* with this function.

Example 2
Eg bare, e' det nokke I veien med deg (I was like, is there something the matter with you?) (Andersen, in press).

Example 3
Und ich so: 'cool!' Und er so: 'hä?' (and I like: 'cool!' and he like: 'what?') (Androutsopoulos, in press).

It is not yet clear whether these developments have occurred simultaneously in each language as loan translations from English, or whether they constitute an extension of what Carstensen (1986) termed 'Euro-English'. Equally, it is not clear whether these are really examples of a youth language, in which case – like the transitory vocabulary of youth slang – they will presumably die out as present-day young people get older, or whether they are examples of a more permanent language change led by younger speakers of the language. In any event, these examples provide a useful bridge between the previous discussion of aspects of young people's social identities through patterns of change and continuity in their English, and the following consideration of the extent to which young people in continental Europe use language to express their multiple identities, and the role English plays in this.

English in Europe

Convery *et al.* (1997) have investigated the extent to which young people in the new Europe have a sense of being European. They found some national differences among the 16–18-year-old students who completed their questionnaire; as Table 2.2 shows, the English students, followed by the French, stand out as different from the German, Italian, Dutch and Spanish respondents in that they claim not to feel particularly European.

Language learning is thought to be a vital aspect of forming a European identity; it is enshrined as such in European Union directives and is

Table 2.2 'Do you think of yourself as being European?' From Convery *et al.* (1997)

	Not at all	*Only partly*	*Yes*
England	39.8	41.6	18.6
France	17.4	40.4	42.1
Germany	8.0	25.6	66.4
Italy	4.3	41.0	54.7
Netherlands	2.6	7.0	90.4
Spain	6.4	25.1	68.4

Table 2.3 Percentage of pupils learning (or having learnt) foreign languages (FLs). From Convery _et al._ (1997)

	One FL	_Two FLs_	_Three FLs_
England	38.1	57.5	4.4
France	0.6	73.3	26.1
Germany	0.8	75.6	23.6
Italy	36.4	51.4	12.1
Netherlands	0.9	1.7	97.4
Spain	88.9	11.1	0
Total	29.8	51.3	18.9

one of the reasons for university Socrates and Erasmus programmes. However, Table 2.3, also from the research of Convery _et al._, shows that feeling European is not necessarily connected to learning languages. Possibly this is so in the case of the Dutch, who were learning three foreign languages and claimed to feel the most European, but the Spanish – the next highest group in self-confessed European identity – learn the lowest number of foreign languages (presumably because some of the language curriculum is taken up with learning the other languages of Spain).

Nevertheless, with the exception of Spain, the majority of young people in the survey were learning at least two foreign languages. What Table 2.3 does not show, however, is that, importantly, the main language that is learned is English. The teaching and learning of English increased dramatically during the second half of the twentieth century (see Dickson and Cumming, 1996), in response to the growing use of English as an international language. This in turn was in large part related to the dominance of the USA politically and economically, a fact reflected in the role that English plays in international youth culture. The popularity of English as a foreign language in European schools means that young Europeans are now much better able to communicate with each other than their parents were. The research of Labrie and Quell (1997) shows this very clearly. When asked which language they would choose to speak to someone from a range of European countries, only a few members of the older age group (over 55) in Greece were able to speak to other Europeans – and then it was mainly only to the British, and only for those Greeks who knew some English. The older French could mainly speak only to people who knew French. There is a consistent pattern in all the European countries where the survey was carried out. The younger age group in all the countries surveyed can speak to more people from more European countries than their parents can but, of course, communication is through English.

It is vital for Europeans to learn each other's languages, rather than for everyone to learn a single lingua franca; yet it is important to note that, like it or not, English does mean that young Europeans are able to speak to each other which will surely give rise to a sense of being European. More relevant, however, is the question of whether English in Europe allows young people to express multiple identities. Is there a pan-European youth identity, expressed, perhaps, with the help of English, like the pan-England youth identity expressed through such features as focus marker *like* and [t] glottaling? Affective factors are thought to be important in the spread of these features in England, and affective factors concerning language are also important for the future of the European Union. Convery *et al.* (1997: 1) argue that 'the long-term success of the European Union and indeed of Europe as a unified whole will depend on present and future younger generations making an emotional as well as rational response to the notion of being European'.

Can English, then, be used to express 'emotional' aspects of young people's social identities? It is clear that young people do use English for some activities specifically associated with emotional reactions; one only has to look at the graffiti in any urban centre in Europe. In Germany English is used in youth magazines as a source for new compounds denoting concepts that can be assumed to have emotive connotations. These compounds are both hybrid (half German and half English), and wholly English. Androutsopoulos (in press) gives examples from young people's magazines which include *Horrorfan, Metallfan, Soundfreak, Drogenfreak, Computer freak, Telefon junkie, Love junkie, Computerfunkie.* Berns (1988: 45) claims that the English used in popular publications for young people creates 'solidarity among speakers and readers by emphasising the shared basis of familiar, although foreign language elements, thus creating an anti-language which distinguishes "us" from "them"'. Preisler (1999) makes a similar argument with reference to use of English by young people in Denmark. He further claims that using English, or a codeswitched variety of English and Danish, is a subcultural practice which embodies a clear value system.

Further evidence of the emotive associations of English comes from Switzerland. Cordey (1997) documented some of the English phrases used as formulae by young speakers of Swiss German dialects: these include *Hi! Cool!* and *Shit!* Her larger study of 220 high-school students in

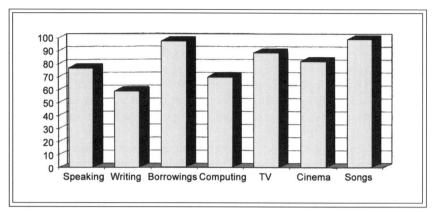

Figure 2.2 Situations in which students may use English (overall percentages). From Cordey (1997)

Fribourg, Switzerland, asked whether they used English in any contexts outside school. Figure 2.2 shows the results of her questionnaire.

The use of English in 'writing' was in letters to English-speaking friends or penfriends; 'speaking' and 'borrowing', however, was not. An example of 'borrowing' is shown in Example 4, from a basketball game recorded in Fribourg. The basketball players were French speakers, consciously using English phrases during their game because, in the words of one of them afterwards, 'c'est cool!'.

Example 4

Let's go les gars ... on y va ... Pierre tu joues playmaker... d'accord moi je vais guard ... eh, look at the ball quand tu coupes ... t'arrives a smasher toi? No problem ... je score d'ou tu veux ... j'ai réussi a facer avec une no-look pass ... it's showtime in LA ... come on ... va au panier avec un power move ... OK give me the ball it's money time.

Particularly clear insight into the connotations that English may have for young Europeans is given from the responses that Cordey received to her question: 'What does the English language represent to you, especially when used in advertisements?' In Switzerland, as in many European countries, English is used extensively in advertising and symbolises a range of meanings (see Cheshire and Moser, 1994). Figure 2.3 shows that 'youth' figured prominently among the most frequent answers Cordey received to this question.

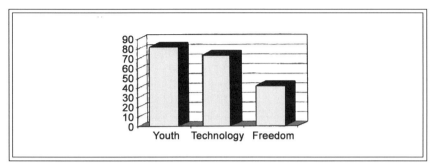

Figure 2.3 Overall percentages of students associating English with youth, technology and freedom. From Cordey (1997)

Interestingly, the Swiss government appears to recognise this association, for during the late 1990s it made use of English in its campaign to discourage driving under the influence of drink or drugs. Large posters by the roadsides showed images of an empty road, with the words 'NO DRINKS – NO DRUGS – NO PROBLEMS'.

Analysis of English in advertisements in French-speaking Switzerland (Cheshire and Moser, 1994) led to the theory that in Switzerland English has lost (or partly lost) its association with an English-speaking country. It was argued that extensive use of English to advertise the most stereotypically Swiss products to Swiss consumers showed English used to symbolise a harmonious Swiss national identity. English is used now so extensively throughout the world that it can serve as an 'open reservoir' for symbolic meanings. It is no longer necessarily associated with a specific English-speaking country. The growing body of research on English in Europe suggests that for young people English can symbolise the international youth culture. This may mean it is associated to some extent with the USA, but youth culture is so multifaceted that it is unlikely to be only the USA (and the association with the USA will in fact be with a range of American subcultures). Nationality is in any case not the main issue; the main point is that English is free to symbolise an international youth culture in the same way that [t] glottaling or theta fronting in England have been divorced from association with London and can now symbolise a pan-regional youth culture in Britain.

'Where We're Going': Trajectories for the New Europe

Use of English in the everyday lives of young people throughout Europe augurs well for the long-term success of Europe as a unified entity. Young people are not only learning English at school, but are also making an emotional response to it. They adapt it so it becomes their own, incorporating it into their national languages by borrowings and codes switching, as in the example from the basketball game in Switzerland, and using it in their leisure activities. They do this in much the same way that young people in England are making an emotional response to the consonant features originating in London, or the Californian features they hear in the broadcast media. Like the adolescents in Reading, Milton Keynes or Hull, young people in Europe are not losing their national or regional identities. Global identities, it seems, are additive, and European adolescents can still express these aspects of their identity through their own first language. Indeed, they can express national (and other) identities through the variety of English they speak. As Graddol (1998: 27) points out, 'Germans will want to sound like Germans when they speak English, not like Britons or Americans'. As with new *like* and the consonant pronunciations, the question of what will happen as the young people get older remains. Presumably when they reach middle age they will no longer see themselves as members of the international youth culture. If nothing else, though, they will know English, and as a result they will be able to talk to other members of the European Union.

This may sound like an argument for using English as a European lingua franca, but this is not the case. It is right to be concerned about the possible domination of English as a lingua franca in Europe, and it is right to insist on a policy of encouraging language learning. Learning a language is also learning a culture, and the citizens of Europe will surely benefit from knowing more about each other's national and regional languages and cultures, and the cultural diversity that exists in each nation-state. But there is little point in pretending the linguistic facts are other than they are. Graddol (1997: 14) claims that Europe is beginning to form a single multilingual area, rather like India, where languages are hierarchically ordered. The 'big' languages (English, French and German) are at the top, with national languages such as Dutch (and, of course, English, French and German) beneath them, while below them are officially recognised and supported languages such as Asturian or Welsh. English, Graddol argues, is set to become more widely used, albeit, as argued above, in varieties that may signal simultaneously national as well as European identity. Equally, although there are many valuable and important reasons for learning other European languages, there is little point in pretending that to feel European it is necessary to learn many European languages. The research of Convery *et al.* (1997) has shown this is not the case. Furthermore, it is possible to express different aspects of identities using any language, or any features of a variety of a language, because given the appropriate set of cultural contexts a language, or a language feature, can become separated from association with its native speakers.

In any case, the concept of the native speaker has no place in the new Europe. Barbour (Chapter 1) argues correctly that the term 'native speaker' is part of a nationalist and monolingual discourse. It is better to deconstruct the term, as Rampton (1995) does, and decompose it into the simple distinction between 'expertise' (skill, proficiency, ability to operate with a language) and 'allegiance' (identification with a language, with the values, meanings and identities that it stands for); see Rampton (1995: 340). Expertise in a language can be acquired, it is not necessarily a skill that one is born with. Expertise in English is being acquired very rapidly by huge numbers of people around the world including, of course, Europe. Allegiance to a language can go hand in hand with allegiance to a nation, by inheritance – this would be the case of the traditional native speaker – but it can also be allegiance by choice. This is the aim of traditional ways of teaching foreign languages such as French or German in Britain, where the language is taught with the literature and the culture of the countries where it is spoken. But allegiance can be to other things as well, which may come with the language not by inheritance but by affiliation. In the case of English this can be to international youth culture or – sometimes – to a specific country, as in Swiss advertisements. There is no reason why it should not, one day, be to Europe.

References

Andersen, G. (in press) *They gave us these yeah, and they like wanna see like how we talk and all that.* The use of *like* and other pragmatic markers in London teenage speech. *Icame.*

Androutsopoulos, J.K. (in press) Grammaticalization in young people's language: The case of German. *Belgian Journal of Linguistics.*

Berns, M. (1988) The cultural and linguistic context of English in West Germany. *World Englishes* 7, 37–49.

Carstensen, B. (1986) Euro-English. In D. Kastovsky and A. Szwedek (eds) *Linguistics Across Historical and Geographical Boundaries.* The Hague: Mouton.

Cheshire, J. (1982) *Variation in an English Dialect: A Sociolinguistic Study.* Cambridge: Cambridge University Press.

Cheshire, J. (1999) Taming the vernacular: Some repercussions for the study of syntactic variation and spoken grammar. *Cuadernos de Filología Inglesa* 8, 59–80.

Cheshire, J. and Edwards, V. (1991) Schoolchildren as sociolinguistic researchers. *Linguistics and Education* 3, 225–49.

Cheshire, J. and Moser, L-M. (1994) English as a cultural symbol: The case of advertisements in French-speaking Switzerland. *Journal of Multilingual and Multicultural Development* 15 (6), 451–69.

Cheshire, J., Edwards, V. and Whittle, P. (1989) A survey of British dialect Grammar. *English Worldwide* 10, 185–225.

Cheshire, J., Kerswill, P. and Williams, A. (1999) *The Role of Adolescents in Dialect Levelling*. Final report to ESRC on project no. R000236180.

Convery, A., Evans, M., Green, S., Macaro, E. and Mellor, J. (1997) An investigative study into pupils' perceptions of Europe. *Journal of Multilingual and Multicultural Development* 18 (1), 1–16.

Cordey, A. (1997) *The English Language in Swiss Advertisements*. Mémoire de licence, Department of English, Université de Fribourg Suisse.

Dailey O'Cain, J. (2000) The sociolinguistic distribution of and attitudes toward focuser *like* and quotative *like*. *Journal of Sociolinguistics* 4, 60–80.

Dickson, P. and Cumming, A. (1996) *Profiles of Language Education in 25 Countries*. Slough: National Foundation for Educational Research.

Foulkes, P. and Docherty, G. (eds) (1999) *Urban Voices: Accent Studies in the British Isles*. London: Arnold.

Graddol, D. (1997) *The Future of English?* London: British Council.

Graddol, D. (1998) Will English be enough? In A. Moys (ed.) *Where Are We Going with Languages?* London: Nuffield Foundation.

Kerswill, P. and Williams, A. (1997) Investigating social and linguistic identity in three British Schools. In U.-B. Kotsinas, A.-B. Stenström and A.-M. Malin (eds) *Ungdomsspråk i Norden. Föredrag från ett forskarsymposium*. Series: MINS. No. 43. Stockholm: University of Stockholm, Department of Nordic Languages and Literature, 159–76.

Labrie, N. and Quell, C. (1997) Your language, my language or English? The potential language choice in communication among nationals of the European Union. *World Englishes* 16 (1), 3–26.

Preisler, B. (1999) Functions and forms of English in a European FL country. In A.R. Bex and R.J. Watts (eds) *Standard English: The Widening Debate* (pp. 239–67). London: Routledge.

Rampton, B. (1995) *Crossing: Language and Ethnicity Among Adolescents*. Harlow: Longman.

Sankoff, G., Thibault, P., Nagy, N., Blondeau, H., Fonollosa, M-O. and Gagnon, L. (1997) Variation in the use of discourse markers in a language contact situation. *Language Variation and Change* 9 (2), 191–218.

Tagliamonte, S. and Hudson, R. (1999) Be like *et al.* beyond America: The quotative system in British and Canadian youth. *Journal of Sociolinguistics* 3, 147–72.

Williams, A. and Kerswill, P. (1999) Dialect levelling: Change and continuity in Milton Keynes, Reading and Hull. In P. Foulkes and G. Docherty (eds) *Urban Voices: Accent Studies in the British Isles* (pp. 141–62). London: Arnold.

Chapter 3

The Lexicon in European Languages Today: Unification or Diversification?

RICHARD TRIM

Are the meanings of words in European languages coming closer together in today's world of mass communication? It would seem that, despite trends such as the continuing internationalisation of lexis in technology, business and politics, the foundations of our languages embodied in long-standing concepts of the lexicon are likely to preserve their own semantic identity. This particularly appears to be the case regarding the figurative lexicon. By examining what has gone on in the past, we are able to have a clearer view of processes operating in the present and what is likely to happen in the future.

Recent studies have shown that many fundamental concepts retain language-specific variants because of time-worn mechanisms in the creation of metaphoric expressions. If the histories of metaphor models are analysed, the on-going cross-fertilisation of meaning which has taken place in past centuries has not prevented a significant proportion of the lexicon choosing paths specific to either one language or group of languages. The suggestion here is that the meanings of many shared concepts will continue to develop a common, cross-language base in their semantic structures but preserve clearly defined conceptual variants.

Findings taken from comparative analyses of metaphor paths suggest two forces are at work: on the one hand, the effect of the language's immediate cultural environment on the conceptualisation of ideas embodied in metaphor models and, on the other, the semantic dynamics of the mental lexicon shared by the language's speakers. To illustrate the principles in operation this study first analyses the flexibility of meaning in metaphor with regard to cultural perception and then examines the history of the 'dryness metaphor model' in the major European languages; this covers a wide range of language-specific meanings. The study suggests that the notion of *intralingual conceptual networking* in the mental lexicon is the principal mechanism at work in networking of this kind. The model provides evidence that networking propagates meaning changes based on underlying clusters which have resulted in either the divergence or extinction of metaphor paths. The implication is that conceptual networking is likely to preserve the identity of individual European languages as far as their basic vocabularies are concerned.

Impressions of Uniformity in European Lexis

Moves towards political unification of an area comprising a number of different languages would suggest that the meanings of words in many fields are likely to come closer together. Even without political unification, a cursory glance at the world of technology suggests that more and more words in European languages are becoming identical in both their structural and semantic components. The huge increase in vocabularies in the field of technology and business since the last war, particularly of English origin, has led to considerable unification in lexical meaning. Multilingual computer dictionaries in information science demonstrate this uniformity as can be seen, for example, in the derivatives of 'information' itself, as illustrated in Table 3.1. Language specialists working with more than one language, however, particularly those working in translation or in the compilation of bilingual dictionaries, are very aware of the variations which can arise in interlingual meaning. The changing nature of the multilingual lexicon is too complex for it to become completely uniform, despite a range of unifying trends.

One area of the European lexicon which is particularly prone to semantic variation is the figurative component. There is also a large

Table 3.1

English	French	German	Italian
information society	société de renseignements	Informations-gesellschaft	societa di informazioni
information processing	traitement de l'information	Informations-verarbeitung	elaborazione di informazioni
information transmission	transmission des informations	Informations-weitergabe	trasmissione di informazioni

Source: *Computer Informatik* Compact Verlag: Munich, 1991

amount of figurative lexis in technical terminology but, although a project is currently under way at Robert Gordon University to examine variation in this field, sufficient data is not yet available to determine whether either literal or figurative concepts reveal a large amount of interlingual semantic variation.

It will be suggested here that there are two main forces at work in maintaining variation. The first involves the flexible nature of conceptual interpretation as portrayed by the culture-dependent perception of the environment. The second is a process I shall term *intralingual conceptual networking* which involves the association of conceptual links in the mental lexicon of a language's speakers. The evolution of metaphoric meaning will be examined; dictionary attestations suggest that a large proportion of a language's figurative vocabulary has been formed as a result of the two processes throughout its history and will continue to do so in the future.

With regard to the first process, the root of multilingual conceptual variation lies in the flexibility of semantic interpretation. The idea of flexibility in both literal and figurative meaning has, nevertheless, been sharply contested in the past both by linguists and philosophers. As far as metaphor is concerned, such views date back to Aristotle's Comparison Theory which implies that metaphoric projection shares a fixed set of features or common category memberships (*Poetics*, xxi, 7ff; *Rhetoric*, III, ii, 7ff). These principles have gone on to form the base of later models such as Richards' (1965) Interactionist View which likewise implies fixed-reference meaning in the metaphor projection, as well as Harris's Anomaly View which suggests that metaphor is a mistake or absurdity, since only literal concepts can portray the truth (Harris, 1976).

Many other fixed-reference models for defining meaning have accompanied these ideas. Included are Fillmore's check-list theory of attributes in semantic categories (Fillmore, 1982) and Putnam's rejection of individual conceptualisation with the argument that the interpretation of meaning has nothing to do with a so-called 'psychological state' (Putnam, 1975: 135–6).

Because of the extreme variation in metaphoric interpretation it became clear that another approach had to be found. The answer came from cognitive psychology in the 1970s which viewed meaning as how the mind interprets it rather than establishing rigid semantic categories. A useful theoretical framework for explaining variational phenomena arose in prototype theory. This approach originally applied to literal meaning and was later transferred to figurative language.

A pioneering experiment in variation of literal meaning involved the conceptualisation of a group of kitchen utensils in which it was found that not all participants in the experiment agreed whether a particular container could be termed a vase, cup, bowl, mug or dish (Labov, 1973: 340). This led to further experiments and to the development of prototype theory which demonstrated that people view some objects as being more typical of a particular semantic category than others and that many definitions of a concept have so-called 'fuzzy-edges'. In our society, a robin would be a typical bird but not necessarily a parrot or ostrich (Rosch, 1975).

If we apply a cross-cultural dimension, flexibility in meaning becomes even more apparent. The 'birdiness' semantic category would have a very different conceptual ordering, for example, what would be a typical bird in the Caribbean or certain parts of Africa? Variation in meaning is increased yet again when this approach is applied to figurative meaning caused by the double conceptualisation process of mapping an image from one semantic domain to another. The existence of two semantic domains played a major role in the effectiveness of metaphor use. The fluctuating interpretation of metaphors appears to depend on the distance between semantic domains and the extent of their individual structures. The idea of how apt the creation of a metaphor is in a given society was proposed by the hypothesis of prototype metaphor by Tourangeau and Sternberg (1982), who found that an increase in similarity within domains tends to favour the degree of aptness in metaphor but between domains it has a negative effect. In other words, 'within-domains dissimilarity' such as 'his feet were stars' or 'between-domains similarity' such as 'wine is whisky' would create difficulties in interpretation (Aitchison, 1992b: 146).

The implication here, as far as intercultural meaning is concerned, is that metaphor involves several types of variables which vary according to personal and cultural interpretation. On the personal level, images in the above examples would be chosen along the scales of the two domains which increase their dissimilarity or similarity, respectively, to make them more apt and suitable metaphors. On the cultural level, one of the semantic categories of world leaders chosen by Tourangeau and Sternberg would vary considerably. Interpretation of leaders from the 1980s, such as Carter and Brezhnev, would vary according to the country.

This represents cultural attitudes towards concepts and is the base of culturally influenced metaphors. The animal category which Tourangeau and Sternberg use in their models is another case in point. Their images vary considerably between one language and another. According to Newmark (1985: 306), horses are strong in English, healthy and diligent in French and possibly hard-working in German, although *Ross* ('steed') tends to be a blockhead. Ducks are affectionate in English but lying rumours in French and German, while hens are prostitutes in French. A tiger is fierce in English and German, but more sly and cunning in French. An elephant never forgets in most European languages except in Russian in which it has no connotations.

Intralingual Conceptual Networking

The second main culture-specific mechanism in operation, once an initial concept is born, is the process of networking which forms its own pattern in each language. Networking is basically related to conceptual organisation in the mind. Because of different associations, words take on various meanings and are linked to specific semantic fields. Recent warfare terminology is an example. The term *task force* used in the Falklands War spread to all kinds of usage in government terminology and the notion of *surgery* as in *surgical bombing* during the Gulf War was networked to many other concepts. Newspapers use this technique every day and, although many associations are simply a play on words, some metaphoric terms become entrenched in the language, giving a word a new meaning. There are four common types of word links in the mental lexicon: coordination (salt, pepper, mustard), collocation (salt, water), superordination (colour + red, blue, green) and synonymy (hungry, starved) (Aitchison, 1992b: 75). These are responsible for the types of lexical chaining which arises in metaphor clusters and are again evidence for the kind of conceptual networking which produces interlingual conceptual divergence.

Some networking models in metaphor start off in isolation with regard to neighbouring languages. Others, particularly in basic concepts, start off with an underlying construct which may span many cultures and even have universal tendencies. Supporters of this idea refer to such constructs as image schemas (Lakoff, 1987: 269ff). A major proportion of these schemas involve spatial orientation such as up-down, centre-periphery, inside-outside structures which are common to human conceptualisation in general and produce similar types of metaphors, for example, *I'm feeling on top of the world* where up = positive/good. This is found in many other European languages, for example, French *haut/bas*, etc. Other image schemas are likewise physiologically based such as emotion embodied in the form of heat and pressure, for example, *he flipped his lid* where pressure = anger (Lakoff, 1987: 385).

These underlying images appear to constitute *metaphor-building blocks*, an idea which is also supported by historical perspective. Identical features, for example, appear to have created similar metaphors over and over again throughout the evolution of Indo-European languages. An example is the verb 'to see' generating the meaning 'to understand' (Sweetser, 1990: 448).

Once core concepts have been established in a language, with or without cross-cultural building-blocks, they can attract a large number of words in the form of metaphoric chaining, for example *mother* linking *mother country, mother tongue,* etc. in the form of collocational associations. An example in French would be chaining the metaphoric adjective *chaud* (hot = controversial) to the noun *dossier* (in the sense of *court-case*) as in, for example, *controversial law-suit.* These links can be built up during the course of time and each language's metaphor models may acquire extensive coverage of a variety of semantic domains. These meanings continue to fluctuate so that new metaphor paths may be created in the model's clusters and old ones become obsolete.

Associations of conceptual links and semantic domains thus become a powerful force in the internal dynamics of semantic evolution. It has been found that one member of a semantic domain may trigger the inclusion of another member. Animal categories once again come to mind. In the bird category, the image *goose* in English acquired the metaphoric meaning of foolishness in the 16th century. This quickly spread to *cuckoo* and *pigeon* and much later, in the 17th and 18th centuries, to *coot* and *turkey* (Lehrer, 1985: 289). The powerful role of semantic domains in meaning transfer is likewise supported by evidence in the semantic change of literal meaning, for example, Stern's (1931) finding that all 23 Old and Middle English adverbs he discovered with the meaning 'rapidly' changed to the sense 'immediately' in a chain reaction over a relatively short time during the Middle Ages. The conclusion here is therefore that networking within a semantic domain may be responsible for meaning transfer.

A final outcome of language-specific patterns is that a language has the tendency to channel metaphoric concepts. There is a certain amount of speculation about why this happens. Apart from the effects of the immediate cultural environment, there may be a covert desire by speakers of a language to keep their mental models consistent (Aitchison, 1992a: 37). A factor which appears to be important is the result of the chaining process. The bigger a metaphor model is, the more opportunity it has to create new related metaphors in a 'snowball effect', demonstrating how existing metaphors are often responsible for new ones. Many of these are in turn slotted into strands and extensions generated from the main channels of core concepts which then follow set paths. A good example of demonstrating how this works and influences mechanisms operating in current conceptual variation is the 'dryness' metaphor model.

Dryness has been chosen for its high level of productiveness in European languages in general. An initial survey of meanings relating to the figurative component of dryness in several European languages (English, French, German, Spanish, Italian and Russian) indicates more than 70 dictionary attestations. More detailed analyses with different etymological dictionaries would probably double that figure. Dryness represents a universal basic concept along with others such as wetness, heat, cold, etc. and, in some respects, is physiological as it can be perceived by touch and has a physical sensation like heat or cold. However, it also differs considerably from heat and cold in that most perception is via sight. As sight tends to produce more conceptual variation, the result is more varied in metaphoric language than concepts such as heat and cold.

An overview of present-day metaphors in European languages confirms this view. In French, *un coup sec* cannot translate literally into English 'a dry movement' or 'dry strike/blow' with the meaning of 'quick and sharp'. Another type of metaphor, or non-metaphoric expression, would have to be found. To explain this feature, a breakdown of the different metaphor groups and a detailed cross-language comparison is required.

With a certain liberty of interpretation, a large proportion of these different meanings can be reduced to a common denominator. It is suggested here that the original concept of dryness is related to the equation of dryness = deficiency. A large percentage of meanings may therefore be related to the notion of 'a lack of something'. When the majority of these meanings is analysed, a common interpretation is that some element is missing.

From this original concept, five main clusters appear to have developed in the form of metaphor building-blocks. The first is the most natural and logical one related to the model's literary meaning component, while the last one represents a miscellany of meanings linked to the notion of deficiency but which cannot be grouped conceptually under one definable concept like the other clusters.

(1) Lack of a liquid.
(2) Lack of feeling or emotion.
(3) Lack of interest/ornamentation.
(4) Lack of life or physical/mental well-being.
(5) Lack of miscellaneous items.

These building-blocks separate into conceptually related sub-groups: for example, cluster (4) has the notion of lacking life so that metaphors are created in the form of Italian *fare secco* 'to make dry = to kill' and *secco* 'dry = dead'; lacking physical well-being as in Russian 'to dry someone = to weaken someone' and 'dry = thin'; or a negative mental state (i.e. lack of mental well-being) as in French *sécher sur ses pieds* (attested 1550) where 'to dry on one's feet' means 'very worried'.

One aspect of multilingual comparison will be selected using English and French. A striking feature which arises in a comparison of these two languages is not only the fact that metaphor productivity is quite different between them but also that French is far more productive. The difference can first be seen in the following samples regarding the first four clusters and which include a sample of dictionary attestations, in current use or archaic (+), through the histories of the two languages.

The higher level of productivity in the French model suggests that the dryness 'groove' in French has been well established throughout its history and is likely to continue to promote metaphor creation along these lines. Additional encyclopedic information reveals that many obsolete metaphor paths in English are caused by the decreasing influence of Latin, which contained many of the missing metaphor groups and passed them on to post-Latin languages; this decrease has not been so well marked in French. Furthermore, French has been the subject of more cultural influence from the Catholic religion, for example, and a number of metaphors in this domain are shared by other Latin languages but much less so by Germanic ones.

Although there are many cross-language links, it is interesting to speculate why there are fundamental conceptual variations between the languages, particularly in modern English and French. French has an over-riding negative quality in the dryness concept which is not really present in modern English. Could this be because of the history of a drier climatic environment in which water is a more precious element? This seems to be reflected in the difference between Germanic and Latin languages in which dryness and wetness have contrasting positive and negative qualities.

British English

He's a bit wet (feeble or inept); 'wets' in the Conservative party (negative attitude towards more liberal tendencies.

German
im Trocknen (in the dry) = under cover
im Trocknen = in safety
hoch und trocken sitzen (to sit high and dry) = to be in safety

One way of highlighting the differing levels of productivity in networks is by examining patterns in current usage through the medium of translation, since this produces an exact picture of which images and combination of images may be used across languages.

Conceptual Combinations in Translation

These networking processes result overall in clear language-specific patterns. Different concepts often have to be used for the same message or multiple metaphor images may not match between languages. To highlight this disparity, it would be useful to give a brief overview of current usage in other lexical terms with regard to translation. Translation demonstrates conceptual divergence very clearly when trying to find cross-language equivalents. The following samples of divergence are taken from translations of news bulletins from the European Parliament and involve variational networks:

Sample A
The metaphor image is not usually used in one language. In this case, the English term 'envelope' has not undergone the same conceptualisation as in French:

network in French: envelope = financial allocation
semantic domains: *commission, gratification, indemnité de départ, pôt-de-vin* (commission, bonus, golden handshake, bribe)
Le rapporteur a obtenu l'appui total de la commission ... pour réclamer une enveloppe globale de 16.300 millions d'écus (5/6/98)
Official translation: The rapporteur received the full backing of the Committee ... by demanding an overall budget of ECU 16,300 million.

Sample B
The metaphor exists in both languages but not according to the same semantic domain:

metaphor network: marriage = merger

French network has more extensive cover regarding semantic domains: (*Mariage de couleurs, parfums, goûts, techniques, entreprises, etc.* Marriage of colours, perfumes, tastes, techniques, companies, etc.)

M. *Van Miert a révélé que le mariage récemment annoncé entre Daimler-Benz et Chrysler ne semblait pas devoir soulever de grand problème* (27/5/98)
Official translation: Mr Van Miert said he saw no great problem with the recently announced Daimler-Benz/Chrysler alliance.

Sample C
The metaphor exists according to the same semantic domain but not in compound images:

compound network:	light = clarification +
equivalence:	jeter une lumière sur ... = throw a light on ...
brutal model:	French network covers more semantic domains:
violent:	*choc, coup, ton, réponse, caractère, discours, article* (shock, blow, tone, reply, character, speech, article)
sudden:	*douleur, attaque, mort* (pain, attack, death)
dramatic:	*hausse, chute, changement, phénomène* (rise, fall, change, phenomenon)
sharp:	*coup de frein, coup d'accélérateur* (braking, accelerating)

Peu après que l'actualité ait jeté une lumière brutale sur les problèmes de la garde des enfants après des divorces d'époux de nationalité différente (16/4/98)
Official translation: Following close on media revelations pointing up the problems over custody of children after divorce between spouses of different nationalities.

It can be seen in these samples that a number of different combinations in conceptual variation can arise when attempting to select the right equivalent in translation. These combinations are a result of differential conceptualisation and variational networks.

In conclusion, it appears that large numbers of metaphors in European languages do not share the same meanings because of cross-cultural variation in the conceptual interpretation of images and language-specific networking patterns. This can be seen from the highly productive dryness model and lack of equivalents in translating metaphoric items. It may therefore be assumed that the European lexicon, at least in its basic vocabulary, will continue to reveal considerable variation in its conceptual structure. Despite unifying trends in borrowing processes and shared cultural features in a world of mass communication, the meanings of words, at least in the figurative lexicon, are unlikely to become uniform. Although this on-going trend will not make the task of teachers, translators or lexicologists any easier, it is surely positive that the languages of Europe will no doubt preserve their own semantic and cultural identities.

References

Aitchison, J. (1992a) Chains, nets or boxes? The linguistic capture of love, anger and fear. In W. Busse (ed.) *Anglistentag, Düsseldorf* (pp. 25–38), Tübingen: Max Niemeyer Verlag.

Aitchison, J. (1992b) *Words in the mind: an introduction to the mental lexicon* (2nd edition). Oxford: Blackwell.

Aristotle (1927) *The Poetics.* In W. Fyfe (trans.) Cambridge, MA: Harvard University Press.

Aristotle (1932) *The Rhetoric of Aristotle.* In L. Cooper (trans.) New York: Appleton-Century-Crofts.

Fillmore, C. (1982) Frame semantics. *Linguistic Society of Korea,* 111–38.

Harris, R. (1976) Comprehension of metaphor: A test of a two-stage processing model. *Bul. Psychon. Soc.* 8, 321–4.

Labov, W. (1973) The boundaries of words and their meanings. In C. Bailey and R. Shuy (eds) *New Ways of Analyzing Variation in English.* Washington, DC: Georgetown University Press.

Lakoff G. (1987) *Women, Fire and Dangerous Things.* Chicago: University of Chicago Press.

Lehrer, A. (1985) The influence of semantic fields on semantic change. In J. Fisiak (ed.) *Historical Semantics and Historical Word-formation* (pp. 283–96). Berlin: Mouton.

Newmark, P. (1985) The translation of metaphor. In: W. Paprotté and R. Dirven (eds) *The Ubiquity of Metaphor* (pp. 195–326). Amsterdam: Benjamins.

Putnam, H. (1975) The meaning of 'meaning'. In K. Gunderson (ed.) *Language, Mind and Knowledge* (pp. 131–93). Minnesota Studies in the Philosophy of Science, Vol. 7. Minneapolis: University of Minnesota Press.

Richards, I. (1965) *The Philosophy of Rhetoric.* New York and London: Oxford University Press.

Rosch, E. (1975) Cognitive representations of semantic categories. *Journal of Experimental Psychology: General* 104 (3), 192–233.

Stern, G. (1931) *Meaning and Change of Meaning.* Bloomington: University of Indiana Press.

Sweetser, E. (1990) *From Etymology to Pragmatics: Metaphorical and Cultural Aspects of Semantic Structure.* Cambridge: Cambridge University Press.

Tourangeau R. and Sternberg, R. (1982) Understanding and appreciating metaphors. *Cognition* 11, 203–44.

Chapter 4

Lost in Translation: EU Language Policy in an Expanded Europe

PAUL GUBBINS

In November 1998 the European Union began formal accession negotiations with six countries: Cyprus, the Czech Republic, Estonia, Hungary, Poland and Slovenia. Provided the negotiations proceed as planned it is possible these countries will become members of the EU in or around the year 2003. They are likely to be followed by other EU applicants, including Bulgaria, Latvia, Lithuania, Slovakia and Romania. By the year 2015 the EU could comprise more than 25 nations, in contrast to the present 15.

Many of the problems associated with expansion have been documented. The principal difficulty is economic: if all current 11 applicants were absorbed into the EU its population would expand by 28% and yet its gross domestic product by a mere 4% (Grabbe and Hughes, 1998: 51). Accordingly, the EU is undertaking vital, possibly overdue reform of financial arrangements such as the Common Agricultural Policy. The European Commission is seeking, for instance, to redirect farm funding in accordance with the 1992 MacSharry reforms by decoupling aid from production volumes.

Changes to reflect an expanded EU and, at the same time, to contain spending, are apparent in other areas. For instance, structural funds governing regional aid are to be directed at a smaller recipient percentage of EU population (some 35% as against the present 50%). Institutional reform is also intended at least partially to cut costs. The 1997 Treaty of Amsterdam includes among other terms an expansion of majority voting and, to avoid a bloated, unworkable and expensive European Parliament, an undertaking that the composition of Parliament be limited to a maximum of 700 members (Bainbridge, 1998: 112) irrespective of the eventual size of the enlarged union. Whether the Parliament, in its

46

present censorious mood,[1] will seek to amend this limitation, remains to be seen.

Nevertheless, despite economic, social and structural preparations for an expanded European Union, of which perhaps the most apparent and, in certain quarters, the most contentious is the introduction of a common currency, there is one significant policy largely ignored by planners and politicians. This is language – no less contentious than the euro and, indeed, because of its innate emotional appeal, probably more so. The link between language and nationality and, by extension, nationalism, accounts at least partially for the reluctance of the European institutional hierarchy to address language policy, which remains mired in the muddy thinking of a European community far smaller and far cosier than the one envisaged in the 21st century.

That EU language policy – such as it is – is nothing more than a shoddy, shambolic charade is painfully evident. Robert Phillipson notes: 'Language policies are often so vague (e.g. the Maastricht Treaty's support for the maintenance of cultural diversity) and abstract that they seem to be divorced both from scientific analysis of what is at stake and from the harsher realities of linguistic hierarchisation' (Phillipson, 1998: 97). Sean O'Riain, ambassador in Warsaw to the Irish Republic, highlights the dichotomy in the EU between 'the fine words about plurilingualism ... and the practice which is anglicisation' ('les belles phrases de plurilinguisme ... et la pratique qu'est l'anglicisation') (Moon and O'Riain, 1998: 98). For Brian Moon, an EU translator, 'there prevails in the EU the sharpest contrast between political declarations and linguistic practice' ('en EU ekzistas la plej granda kontrasto inter politikaj deklaroj kaj lingva praktiko') (Moon and O'Riain, 1998: 99).

The political declarations to which Moon refers are expressed perhaps most succinctly in a resolution of the Council of the European Union passed on 16 December 1997. The council felt that 'proficiency in several Community languages has become a precondition if citizens of the European Union are to benefit from the occupational and personal opportunities open to them in the border-free Single Market.'[2] In addition, the resolution noted the principle of 'equal status for each of the languages of the union' and added that this 'may, in the medium term, enable each citizen to have access to the cultural wealth rooted in the linguistic diversity of the union' (Notice 98/C1/02).

Noble sentiments – but observance of linguistic diversity, let alone language equality, lies rather in the breach than in the practice. Indeed, not even the European Parliament implements the 1997 resolution. The MEP Olivier Dupuis, while acknowledging a *de jure* equality of languages, notes a *de facto* parliamentary reality where 'in more and more sessions – of a less official nature – interpreting is not assured or is not assured in all languages and the members or officials use French and, to an increasing degree, English' ('dans de plus en plus de réunions – moins officielles – l'interprétation n'est pas assurée ou n'est pas assurée dans toutes les langues et les parlamentaires ou les fonctionnaires utilisent le français et, dans une mesure croissante, l'anglais') (Dupuis, 1998: 103).

Furthermore, in certain areas of EU activity many languages are excluded. The European Observatory on Drugs and Drug Addiction in Lisbon uses English, French and Portuguese, while the European Agency for the Environment in Copenhagen uses solely English (Dell'Alba, 1998a: 35). Over-reliance on English, whatever the practicalities, is nevertheless impossible to reconcile with the declared notion of equal status for all EU languages and is potentially damaging to future harmonious cooperation in Europe. For instance, on 1 September 1997 the French newspaper *Le Figaro* recorded its displeasure that the French version of the Treaty of Amsterdam was available only ten days after ratification and contained error and inexactitude. The newspaper also complained that the English text of the treaty was regarded in Brussels as the official version (see Masson, 1999).

Choice of language, too, mocks linguistic equality and leads to irritation and squabbling. On 2 July 1999, under the headline 'Language "snub" infuriates Berlin', the British newspaper *The Guardian* reported a German threat to boycott meetings of European industry ministers conducted during the Finnish presidency of the EU. The Germans objected that translation would be provided only in English, French and Finnish. In rebutting the Germans, the Finnish prime minister, Paavo Lipponen, unwittingly voiced the dilemma at the core of EU language policy: 'If one language gets a favoured position then others will ask for the same treatment.' Indeed so: if, in this instance, English, French and Finnish are so favoured, then why not others?

If this is an accurate reflection of current language policy – an alliance of pious pretence and parlous pragmatism – what chance is there for language equality in an expanded Europe, which could see the present 11 official languages increase to 22 or, according to some estimates, as many as 26 (Dell'Alba, 1998a: 35)? Perhaps the European Union should abandon its stated objective of linguistic equality, and honestly and openly embrace English as an institutional lingua franca. This would at least reflect European reality as perceived by Cay Dollerup who, while noting it will require more than a generation for English to be used as second or 'other' language in the everyday life of a member state, adds that 'in securing adequate, if not perfect communication between democratic states ... it may well be on the way to becoming the common European working language – outside the institutionalised European Union' (Dollerup, 1996: 36). Whatever the truth of this assertion, the German threat to boycott ministerial meetings conducted without the German language (quoted above) is indicative that English will not always prevail. Prowess in a foreign language is one thing; pride in a native language another. It is unlikely English will become 'the common European working language' (Dollerup), whether inside or outside the institutionalised EU, without considerable opposition (particularly from numerically strong and economically powerful languages such as German).

A Socratic Solution

A more equitable solution to the language dilemma might be found in a resolution of the Council of Ministers who, in welcoming the Socrates programme (successor to, among others, the Erasmus and Lingua programmes), argued that school pupils 'should as a general rule have the opportunity of learning two languages of the Union other than their mother tongue(s) for a minimum of two consecutive years.'[3] The ministers added that 'provision of teaching for languages which are less widely used or less frequently taught should be increased and diversified as far as possible, at all levels and throughout all types of curricula' (95/C207/04).

However, as pointed out elsewhere,[4] young Europeans financed under Erasmus and Lingua remained unmoved by efforts to promote less widely used languages. In 1993 the United Kingdom was the most popular destination for students on those schemes, with France in second place. In addition, the impact of Erasmus and Lingua was limited: a mere 1.5% of eligible young Europeans benefited from the programmes.

There is no reason to believe Socrates will change that position. Indeed, because of EU expansion and ensuing constraints on spending (see above), the situation is likely to deteriorate. It is all very well for EP-rapporteur Doris Pack to trumpet Socrates as 'the success story of the European Union';[5] both reality and eventuality indicate a different, more pessimistic scenario resulting, as much as anything else, from lack of adequate funding. Thus in October 1997 MEPs appealed to the European Commission for a substantial increase in Socrates funding. Parliament wanted to expand the existing 850 million ecu budget by an additional 100 million; even this would have been substantially less than the 1005 million originally proposed for a union of 12 members.[6] In a debate on Socrates funding one MEP, Dietrich Elchlepp, dubbed its financing 'scandalous' (4-507/178). Another MEP, Eluned Morgan, speaking in a subsequent debate, addressed herself to the problems facing Socrates in a widening Europe:

> The programme is being expanded to the ten associated countries of central and Eastern Europe. The budgetary effects of this expansion have to be considered. We originally ordered a set meal for our family of 12 people. We then invited 12 more people to the table but I am afraid we did not order any extra food. What we need is more resources for our caterer to ensure that none of our family or our guests leaves our educational table unfed or hungry. Our citizens have an educational and cultural appetite. We must try to make sure those appetites are satisfied (4-507/177-78).

The eloquence was in vain. The commissioner responsible for Socrates, Edith Cresson, declared her sympathy for the views expressed in the debate but reminded MEPs of the need for austerity. She permitted a mere 0.5% increase in funding for 1997–98 which was in line with budgetary expansion for other internal policies of the EU.

The Radical Approach

It was because of these various issues – the gulf between linguistic policy and practice; absence of significant language equality and the resultant democratic tensions; the cost of supporting not only a creaking programme such as Socrates but also, more significantly, translation and interpreting in a union set to embrace some 25 countries – that prompted the Italian-based Radical Party to take a fresh look at EU language policy and to engender much-needed debate on the subject. As the Radical Party MEP Gianfranco Dell'Alba – sitting in the European Parliament as a member of the European Radical Alliance – states in his working document on (non)-communication in the European Union put to the EP Committee for Institutional Affairs in August 1997: 'If there is one important and urgent issue in the process of European integration on which there is a guilty and embarrassed silence it is undoubtedly that of (non)-communication in the Union' (Dell'Alba, 1998a: 34). A parallel document issued by the Radical Party warns bluntly that 'lack of a lasting solution for the language problem may threaten long term political cohesion of the European Union' (Dell'Alba, 1998b, 37).

The Dell'Alba working document examines various methods of international communication, including the so-called Swiss or Scandinavian system by which everyone uses his or her own language but has sufficient aural skills to understand the other tongues being spoken. This system is dismissed as impractical where more than three languages are involved. The document looks too at the multinational system, i.e. adoption of one language (usually English) used for formal communication by all partners; this method was imposed in the former Soviet Union with Russian as lingua franca. The document also considers practice in both the United Nations and the European Union in which the prevailing principle is inequality. Many languages are excluded as 'non-official', some are included as 'official', and of these one or two are more official, or more equal, than others.

The Dell'Alba document also gives a breakdown of interpreting and translation costs in the various institutions of the European Union. This is welcome, although should possibly be treated with caution. Clear and comprehensible information on interpreting and translation is as difficult to extract from the European Union as courtesy from a double-glazing company. Indeed, not even MEPs are entirely successful in coaxing facts from bureaucrats. On 5 January 1999 Eryl McNally MEP tabled the following entirely unambiguous written parliamentary question: 'Could the Commission please tell me the total cost of interpretation and translation fees within the Institutions of the European Union?'[7] The response was a fudge.

With commendable speed – one might say improper haste – a reply was forthcoming two days later. While the McNally question quite distinctly requested the costs for all EU institutions, the writer of the letter, a certain Julian Priestley, limited himself solely to the European Parliament and specifically to interpreting. While acknowledging that 'the cost of multilingualism for an institution such as the EP could represent up to 30% of its operating budget' (letter of 7 January 1999, ref. 000516), Priestley then sought to minimise this figure by concluding that 'the cost of interpretation staff overall can therefore *presumably* [my italics] be put at some 4.7% of Parliament's budget of some ECU 900m.'

It should be noted that the letter brushes aside the cost of translation, for which neither staffing nor operating statistics are provided. Little wonder, perhaps, when the figure given for interpreting staff is merely presumed to be 4.7%. One can perhaps sense the current anger and frustration of members of the EP when faced with lax accounting of which this is possibly just one example.

Nevertheless the 30% of the parliamentary budget quoted by Priestley for total interpreting and translation costs (including not just language staff but 'secretarial costs, the cost of printing and transporting documents ... and costs relating to rooms, interpreters' booths and control booths' (Priestley letter)) corresponds to figures quoted by Dell'Alba for other institutions of the union (see Table 4.1). It should be noted that the amounts relate to 1996 and cover 11 official languages of the union. The first column shows the total budget for the appropriate institution in millions of ECU and the second the percentage of that budget spent on servicing those 11 languages. The relatively low figure for the European Parliament is explained, according to Dell'Alba, by changes in accounting techniques (another example, perhaps, of EU fudge) – as he puts it: 'a change in dimension ... and a new budget layout which has markedly reduced the visibility of the budget headings for expenditure on translation and interpreting' (Dell'Alba, 1998a: 34). At this point one begins to wonder whether apparent accounting niceties are not a deliberate attempt to conceal the truth about EU language costs.

The significance of these figures for an expanded Europe is enormous. As Dell'Alba points out, the present 110 language combinations (11 official languages rendered into each of the remaining 10 languages) could well become anything up to 600 whereby 'the present system could well be brought to collapse' (Dell'Alba, 1998a: 35). At the same time, a potential five- or sixfold corresponding increase in the union's multilingual budget is a nonsense under present or foreseeable economic circumstances. In addition, the use even of as many as 25 official languages in an expanded community makes no allowance for so-called regional or minority languages (such as Catalan, Frisian, Galician or Welsh) spoken by more than 40 million EU citizens (Dell'Alba, 1998a: 35).

Table 4.1 EU language costs (1996)

	Budget (ECU m.)	Interp./transl. %
Parliament	884	12
Commission	307	11
Council	105	32
Court of Justice	43	35
Court of Auditors	19	34
Econ. & Social Cte.	158	29

The Case for Esperanto

To break this *Teufelskreis* of language inequality and 'costs ... which will further increase sharply following future enlargements whilst the quality [of interpreting and translation] will still remain questionable' (Dell'Alba, 1998a: 35), the working paper proposes two possible solutions both based on the idea of a common language. Either, argues Dell'Alba, adopt a single working language from among official tongues of the union (Spanish is suggested supposedly because of alleged ease of learning) or else take a neutral language (and thus offend none of the peoples whose language was not adopted) such as Esperanto. As Dell'Alba says: 'Such a system would ... permit a considerable reduction in the number of interpreters (two per booth instead of the present three or four, or five or six following any enlargements). As regards translation the lingua franca could also be used as the reference language (legal and semantic in a broad sense)' (Dell'Alba, 1998a: 35).

The choice of Esperanto as a potential solution for the language issue is courageous. Declaring oneself an Esperantist is akin to 'coming-out'. The Esperantist often faces mockery and opprobrium from a world unable and unwilling to countenance a language which does not conform with established patterns. Esperanto is 'queer'; it is identifiable neither with a geographical nor with a recognisable sociological entity (the example of Hebrew which, over the centuries, existed without the credibility of a nation-state is conveniently forgotten). It is perceived as artificial, unnatural (as if language is organic and must be 'natural', whatever that might mean); what is unnatural about the word *tablo* (table) beggars belief. Detractors of Esperanto, in condemning the language as unnatural, presumably shun cars or trains whose artificiality must appear a godless affront to the natural act of walking. The absurdity and pettiness of much of the often ill-informed criticism of Esperanto become plain when contrasted to the cultural achievements of the language, a point not lost on the poetry journal *PN Review*. In reporting the nomination of Esperanto poet William Auld for the Nobel literature prize the journal commented that this 'implies that Esperanto, recently accepted by PEN International as a "literary language", has come of age' (*PN Review*, (1998) 25/2: 2).

The Dell'Alba working paper, a valiant attempt to focus attention on a neglected area of EU policy, led to two debates conducted by the European Parliament's Committee on Institutional Affairs (Commission C15) comprising 40 MEPs. The debates were initiated by Dell'Alba and took place in January and February 1998. The debates, while inconclusive, at least broadened discussion on language issues and aired views other than those expressed by the Radical Party.

The overall impression emerging from the debates, however, is the very point of the Dell'Alba initiative: namely, there is sympathy for the language issue but no clear solution to it. This is apparent from the proposals put forward in the debates in which, significantly, the Esperanto option appears a non-starter. For Andreas Manzella, a lingua franca adopted in Europe 'could not be an artificial language ... it must be a living language'.[8] This demonstrates complete misunderstanding of Esperanto which is patently a living language. Similar ignorance of Esperanto was displayed by colleague Antoinette Spaak who claimed: 'Esperanto is not a language based on culture. This bothers me.' Another MEP, Ursula Schleicher, doubted Esperanto's ability to express everyday terms, including those of a technical nature. Contact with Esperanto-speakers would confirm that Esperanto is as capable – or as incapable – in this respect as any other language.

Instead of Esperanto, parliamentarians made other suggestions. Maria Izquierdo Rojo proposed sign-language; Ursula Schleicher – no doubt reflecting her own school experiences but at the same time indicating how out of touch elected representatives can be – proposed Latin. She claimed: 'We already had a language, which no longer exists: Latin, *which we all learned* [my italics]. ... One cannot say that Latin is incomprehensible.' Unfortunately, it is unlikely Ms Schleicher saw *The Guardian* of 1 January 1999 which ran an article stating that 'there seems to be no consensus on how to write 1999 in Roman numerals' ('MM minus I bugs Roman scholars').

Inevitably, some speakers in the debate, such as Karl Schwaiger, sided with the option of English for international usage but – perhaps with an eye to the ballot box – local or regional languages for local or regional use. Charlotte Cederschold argued for English plus one other community language – all very well but of no assistance to the Spaniard who opts to learn French and subsequently works in Ireland. Surreptitious or, indeed, official adoption of English as a European lingua franca would lead, as Dell'Alba pointed out in the debates, to parliamentarians abandoning the very bastion (of linguistic diversity) they seek to defend.

As an aside, it should be noted that no reference was made to Europanto, the apparently rule-free *Mischmasch* of European languages which, according to reports, was launched as a joke by Brussels-based Italian-born translator Diego Marani but which has acquired something of a cult status because of Europanto columns in Swiss and Belgian newspapers. Despite claims that 'dank aan Europanto ... du can communicare mit el mundo entiero zonder need de una foreigna lingua te apprendre',[9] the Europanto edifice collapses when it is remembered that, to appreciate it, at least passing knowledge of several European tongues is mandatory. What is fashionably acceptable for polyglot Brussels and the chattering classes of middle Europe is unlikely to find favour at the factory gates of monoglot Milan or Manchester.

The debates conducted in the Committee for Institutional Affairs, while reaching no firm conclusion, appeared to scupper the flagship of the Radical Party, the pursuance of the Esperanto option. Nevertheless, support for Esperanto in the European Parliament appears strong; one-fifth of MEPs answered 'yes' when asked if they believed Esperanto could help solve the language problems of the European Union (see Table 4.2). The statistics, culled from research by Germain Pirlot, are valid as of 20 January 1999 and, like all statistics, should be treated cautiously. Levels of support for the language may reflect the strength or otherwise of national Esperanto associations and their ability to lobby MEPs, rather than inherent support for Esperanto. Indeed, if 20% of MEPs favour Esperanto, why was there not corresponding support for it in the Dell'Alba initiated debates? According to Pirlot, six of of the 40 members of the Committee for Institutional Affairs had declared themselves for Esperanto (15% of committee membership compared with 20% for all parliamentarians). Pirlot himself, however, is not surprised at the inability of so-called supporters of Esperanto to champion the cause: 'Let us not forget that in general MEPs know very little about Esperanto, since Esperanto-speakers do not think – do not dare – to inform them of the true potential of the language.'[10]

Table 4.2 EP support for Esperanto (by party grouping)

Political grouping	Members	Esp. 'Yes'	Percentage
Union for Europe	35	13	37.14
Greens	27	9	29.62
Liberals, Democrats, Reform	42	10	23.8
Socialists	214	53	24.76
Radical Alliance	20	4	20.0
People's Party (C. Dem)	202	35	17.32
United/Nordic Green Left	34	5	14.7
Indeps. Europe of Nations	15	1	6.66
Non-aligned	37	2	5.4
TOTAL	626	131	20.92

Table 4.3 MEP support for Esperanto (by country)

Member state	MEPs	Esp. 'Yes'	Percentage
Ireland	15	14	93.33
Belgium	25	18	72
United Kingdom	87	30	34.48
Italy	87	19	21.83
Sweden	22	4	18.18
Luxembourg	6	1	16.66
France	87	14	16.09
Spain	64	10	15.62
Austria	21	3	14.28
Finland	16	2	12.5
Portugal	25	3	12
Germany	99	10	10.1
Netherlands	31	2	6.45
Denmark	16	1	6.25
Greece	25	0	0
TOTAL	626	131	20.92

The proportion of MEPs from each country who appear to favour Esperanto breaks down according to statistics in Table 4.3. It is interesting that a third of euro-sceptic Britain's representatives seem to support Esperanto. Perhaps the apparent enthusiasm among native speakers of English (cf. the Irish statistics) reflects a 'guilty conscience' that they enjoy a natural advantage through ready command of English and is an attempt to express sympathy with colleagues whose English has been acquired the hard way. Further research is required to ascertain MEPs' reasons for support of Esperanto.

It should be noted that the Esperanto movement is quick to seize on Pirlot's statistics as evidence for interest in the language which, as seen above, is not confirmed in practice. Such figures tend to give Esperanto-speakers false optimism about the future of their language and are sometimes used – whether mischievously or in good faith – for propaganda purposes. They should perhaps be added to the myths recently exposed by Ziko Marcus Sikosek (1999) by which Esperanto-speakers are prone to delude themselves.

Clearly, despite the Dell'Alba initiative, the European jury is still considering its verdict on language policy. It would seem those responsible for shaping and formulating the Europe of the next century, an expanded Europe, with many new languages to be considered, prefer to adopt an attitude of wait-and-see. Whether future generations will thank them for their perhaps understandable hesitation remains to be seen. It would appear, therefore, that while an expanding Europe seeks new identity and purpose, its definition and expression are doomed to remain lost in translation.

Notes

1. On 14 January 1999 the European Parliament refrained by 293 votes to 232 from censuring the European Commission over budgetary and other irregularities in the Brussels bureaucracy. See for instance *The Guardian* (15 Jan. 1999).
2. Notice 98/C1/02, *Official Journal of the European Communities (Information and Notes)*, 3 Jan. 1998 (European Union, 1998).
3. Notice 95/C207/04, *Official Journal of the European Communities (Information and Notes)*, 12 Aug. 1995 (European Union, 1995).
4. See my article (1996) Sense and Pence: an Alternative Language Policy for Europe. In C. Hoffmann (ed.) *Language, Culture and Communication in Contemporary Europe* (124–31). Clevedon: Multilingual Matters.
5. Debate 4-507, *Official Journal of the European Communities (Debates of the European Parliament)*, 22 Oct. 1997 (European Union, 1997).
6. Debate 4-502, *Official Journal of the European Communities (Debates of the European Parliament)*, 12 June 1997 (European Union, 1997).
7. Correspondence in my possession forwarded by Eryl McNally MEP (for whose help I am grateful).
8. All quotes relating to the committee debates of 27 January and 26 February 1998, are my translations of an Esperanto version published before availability of official transcripts.
9. Leader in *The Guardian*, 6 February 1999: 'Europanto ist uno melangio van de meer importantes Europese linguas ... .'
10. Private letter of 19 March 1999 from Germain Pirlot to the author.

References

Bainbridge, T. (1998) The Treaty of Amsterdam. In M. Fraser (ed.) *Britain in Europe* (pp. 109–12). London: Strategems Publishing.
Dell'Alba, G. (1998a) For an agenda 2000 of European communication. In *The Radical Party* (pp. 34–6). Rome: Partito Radicale.
Dell'Alba, G. (1998b) Proposal of resolution on the communication within the institutions and between the citizens of the union. In *The Radical Party* (p. 37). Rome: Partito Radicale.
Dollerup, C. (1996) English in the European Union. In R. Hartmann (ed.) *The English Language in Europe* (pp. 24–36). Europa 2, 3. Oxford: Intellect.

Dupuis, O. (1998) Langue et démocratie dans l'union européene. In M. Fettes and S. Bolduc (eds) *Towards Linguistic Democracy* (pp. 103–6). Rotterdam: UEA.

European Union (1995) *Official Journal of the European Communities (Information and Notes)*. Brussels: EU.

European Union (1997) *Official Journal of the European Communities (Debates of the European Parliament)*. Brussels: EU.

European Union (1998) *Official Journal of the European Communities (Information and Notes)*. Brussels: EU.

Grabbe, H. and Hughes, K. (1998) EU enlargement: Costs and opportunities. In M. Fraser (ed.) *Britain in Europe* (pp. 50–3). London: Strategems Publishing.

Masson, H. (1999) La angla unuavice (English first). *RetEventoj*, 159. January 1999 (via internet).

Moon, B. and O'Riain, S. (1998) Diskuto. In M. Fettes and S. Bolduc (eds) *Towards Linguistic Democracy* (pp. 98–100). Rotterdam: UEA.

Phillipson, R. (1998) Language policies: Towards a multidisciplinary approach. In M. Fettes and S. Bolduc (eds) *Towards Linguistic Democracy* (pp. 95–7). Rotterdam: UEA.

Pirlot, G. (1999) EU-Statistics. Internet, 27 January 1999.

PN Review (1998) News and Notes, 25/2, Nov/Dec.

Sikosek, Z.M. (1999) *Esperanto sen mitoj*. Antverpeno: FEL.

Chapter 5

Identity in Transition: Cultural Memory, Language and Symbolic Russianness

HARALD HAARMANN

Symbolic Russianness seems familiar to westerners because for centuries, as a result of constant stereotyping, we have constructed a generalising picture of Russia and her culture. Yet in reality our knowledge of Russia, the Russians and their language is more of a fantasyland entirely lacking authenticity. Our picture of Russianness seems no longer familiar when confronted with the reality of changes in Russia's most recent history.

At this point certain questions need to be posed. Is Russian culture in turmoil because Sovietism allegedly stifled traditional patterns of Russianness? Is cultural memory among Russians of today capable of reconstructing symbolic Russianness without the distortions of Sovietism? Has the Russian language the flexibility to adapt to the changes in its political status and to modernise its internal structures? Are Russians capable of constructing the new multinational Russia in cooperation with non-Russian peoples in the Russian Federation? Or, finally, are we witnessing a growing trend toward confrontation as in the case of the recent Chechen-Russian conflict?

The outsider who penetrates Russian political symbolism will sooner or later encounter the idea of Mother Russia (Russian *Rodina-mat'*) and related concepts of femaleness. A recent pronouncement on Russian culture highlighted the special affection for the soil, interpreted here in its geographical function: 'For a long time Russian culture has considered freedom and expanse the greatest aesthetic and ethical blessing of mankind. Now look at the map of the world: the Russian plain is the largest on earth. Did the plain determine Russian character, or did the Eastern Slavic tribes settle on the plain because it suited their spirit?'

(Likhachev, 1991: 10). Any attempt to provide an answer is fruitless because the question is too simplistic. When the eastern Slavic tribes settled on the Russian plain it was peopled by others, a pre-Slavic population. Hence it would be more appropriate to ask: Did the spirit of the pre-Slavic population on the Russian plain suit the Slavs? To help explain the popularity of the Mother Russia theme, the investigation must also touch on the manifold contacts of Russians with non-Russians. Russia has been home to more than 120 nationalities of differing ethnic stock and diversified linguistic affiliations, and with the most varied cultural traditions (i.e. Indo-Europeans, Uralians, indigenous peoples of the Caucasus, Turkic, Mongolian and Palaeoasiatic peoples). Closer examination of the notion 'Mother Russia' reveals that this basic concept assumes, in fact, a multitude of facets.

In his astute assessment of post-communist society in eastern Europe, Tismaneanu (1998) highlights the role of political mythology in the former Eastern bloc countries. Following the revolutionary turmoil of 1989–91, political myth-making filled the void which originated with the demise of Leninism and Sovietism. In Russia, in particular, fantasies of salvation dominated both public debate and private attitudes, and political myth-making flourished in various forms. These include a 'resurrection Utopia' founded on the expectation of a 'great leader' (Perón, Stalin, Hitler or even Putin), on the inclination towards vindictive and messianic mythologies, on scapegoating (modern forms of fascism and anti-semitism), the decommunisation dream, the quest for political justice and a 'velvet counterrevolution', to which dissidents and dreamers of different political colour contribute. However, one major item of Russian political identity is missing from Tismaneanu's kaleidoscopic analysis: the revival of symbolic Russianness through traditional stereotypes. Thus Hellberg-Hirn observes: 'In the post-Soviet Russia of today, however, rich symbolic flora representing an intermixing of codes of popular, ethnic and Imperial Russianness has emerged to fill the value vacuum left by the collapse of the Soviet system' (1998: 1).

The interrelation of stereotypical features in symbolic Russianness, such as soil (Russian *zemlia*) and soul (Russian *dusha*) – 'Mother Russia' and the 'Russian soul', draws heavily on tradition known for centuries from literary, oral and folkloric Russian sources. At first glance, femaleness associated with the country, Russia, may be invoked merely by grammatical gender: *Rossiia* is feminine, as are many names of countries in Slavic or Romance languages (e.g. Slovenia, Bulgaria, Romania, Moldova, Italia, la France, España, Argentina). However, the implications of feminine gender for national identity are more deeply rooted in Russia compared with other countries where gender in the name of the nation-state also recalls 'motherland' (rather than fatherland). 'Mother Russia' is a highly sentimental connotation of the protective spirit inherent in motherly attitudes and behaviour. The allegory of earth as caring mother originated in a society where village life was intrinsically linked with the soil. As a social institution, the self-governing village community (Russian *sel'skaia obshchina*) among the eastern Slavs is older than any state organisation (Danilova, 1994).

In a society where, since the early Middle Ages, the fate of the ordinary individual depended on social bondage, which in practice meant bondage with the soil, the fantasy of salvation is likely to be soil-bound. 'Mother Russia' nourishes her children and gives them shelter, while the vastness of her geographical expanse provides an obstacle to any aggressor such that no enemy could ever entirely conquer her. Moreover, all Russian words for natural features which are of feminine gender are imbued with the same spirit that governs the symbolism of Russian soil. This is true, for example, of Russian *ravnina*, 'plain', or for the female allegorising of rivers. In folk songs, the river Volga is addressed as *mat' rodnaia*, 'birth-giving mother', or *Volga-matushka*, 'Volga – dear mother' (Arutiunian, 1992: 405).

It is hardly surprising for us, as westerners, that soil and soul are essential in understanding not only traditional but also modern Russianness, because for generations we have accepted traditional stereotypes about Russian national identity. From inside Russia, however, this is extraordinary, since for decades concepts such as 'Mother Russia' and 'Russian soul' were excluded from public consciousness as a result of Soviet ideology. This attempt to rupture the traditional patterns of symbolic Russianness ultimately failed, and the question now needs to be asked why, in establishing the cultural identity of the post-Soviet era, there is a renaissance of the tradition across public and private life. To answer the question, the terms 'traditional' and 'tradition' will be used frequently; reference to tradition can hardly be ignored, since Russian culture is rightly understood as 'a culture pathologically committed to tradition' (Goscilo, 1995: 70).

Cultural Stereotyping

To implement Leninism in the emergent Soviet society of the 1920s, older patterns of social, cultural and national or political identification were discarded and replaced by egalitarian ideology. From the start it was difficult to balance the interests, both sentimental and practical, of the multitude of ethnic groups in the Soviet Union (Lewis, 1972; Haarmann, 1995). Up to the *coup d'état* of October 1917, which was actually not a revolution, Russian had been the dominant cultural vehicle in the Russian empire and had exerted considerable pressure on many smaller non-Russian language communities.

Soviet ideologists tried to deconstruct the former overall dominance of Russian by highlighting the new state as a union of equal nationalities, where non-Russians enjoyed equal status with Russians. This ideological egalitarianism became apparent in the name for the new Soviet state. Any association with previous names (Russian Empire, Tsarist Empire), which referred to the ethnic component 'Russian' and the older name 'Russia' (*Rossiia*), was avoided. The name of the new state, the Union of Soviet Socialist Republics (USSR), was an ideological construct, as was the name for the new core land, the Russian Soviet Federative Socialist Republic (RSFSR) – in Russian *Russkaia Sovetskaia Federativnaia Sotsialisticheskaia Respublika*. Highlighting the federative character of the Russian republic emphasised the presence of numerous non-Russian nationalities sur- rounded by Russian settlers: such non-Russians included the Tatars, Mordvins, Mari, Udmurts and Germans in the Volga region; the Kalmyks, Avars, Kabardins and Chechens in the Caucasus; the numerous Samoyedic and Palaeoasiatic peoples in western and northern Siberia; and the Buryats, Yakuts and Evenki in southern Siberia.

The Russian Federation was only one of a number of Soviet republics, but it was the republic with the largest geographical expanse, the most numerous population and the greatest number of individual nation- alities. The other Soviet republics (SSRs – Soviet Socialist Republics) were named after non-Russian nationalities whose populations were concentrated in the respective territories. Among these titular nationali- ties were the Ukrainians (in the Ukrainian SSR), the Belorussians (in the Belorussian SSR), the Armenians (in the Armenian SSR) and the Georgians or Grusinians (in the Georgian SSR).

The new political terminology was not only meant to replace the older nomenclature but was also used to eradicate older bonds of social and cultural identification. The stereotype of 'Mother Russia' was abandoned because of its 'chauvinistic-nationalistic' allure. In forging the identity of the new Soviet society, the homeland of Soviet citizens (i.e. Russians and non- Russians) was officially no longer associated with protective femaleness. In a country where ideology professed egalitarian status for men and women, administration and party bureaucracy were dominated by male functionaries (*apparatchiks*, 'members of the apparatus'). The androcratic tradition of public office in Tsarist Russia continued into Soviet society.

Soviet ideologists were not interested in emphasising the importance of homeland since internationalism was a cornerstone of Leninist doctrine. The communist activist was supposed to strive for world revolution. In this idealistic view, old-fashioned ideas of 'homeland' had no place. Soviet society was perceived as a motor for achieving solidarity with an international proletariat, Soviet territory as a springboard for the spread of revolutionary movements. However, ideology was overtaken by political reality; Stalin's administrative and cultural centralism favoured isolationist, Russian-dominated politics. It was then, in the 1930s, that one of the major paradoxes of Sovietism emerged, the assimilation of pre-Soviet ideas to lend internationalistic ideology a populist touch. As Kelly (1998) notes:

> An especially striking illustration of such assimilation was Stalinist nationalism's governing symbol of *Rodina-mat'* (Mother Russia). This term drew most effectively on popular feeling for the 'home patch' *(rodina* having the original sense of 'birthplace', or 'native village'; the tsarist term for Russia, *otechestvo,* had no such popular resonance). ... It also resonated with the still older respect for *Mat' syra zemlia* (Mother Damp Earth), that is, for the land as giver of life (130f).

Once the Soviet Union came under pressure during the Second World War, the idea of Mother Russia as the homeland for Soviet citizens was revived. In Autumn 1941, as German troops advanced on Moscow, Stalin declared his 'Great War of the Fatherland', the *Velikaia Otechestvennaia Voina,* to rouse the Soviet spirit in defence of the home country. Although the term drew on male heroism, the *Rodina* was also emphasised. After the war was won, the former allies of the Soviet Union became ideological enemies or, to be more exact, were scapegoated as enemies of the working class by the Stalinist perversion of communism. During the 1940s and 1950s, as the Soviet Union isolated herself from the rest of the world, internationalistic ideology lost its grip and the revered concept of *Rodina* gained in public status.

During rebuilding in the western Soviet Union, which had been ravaged between 1941 and 1944, pride in defeating the aggressor and memories of war-time deprivation assumed a novel pattern which was only in part still Soviet. The war memorials erected in the 1960s, most of them large-scale monuments, reflect a female protective identity which even Soviet ideology could not prevent. Since the Orthodox church had been marginalised and the Virgin Mary, as protectress, was no longer in the public domain, there remained only Mother Russia as embodiment of the protective spirit, and this is apparent in the monuments. Perhaps the most famous is the 52-metre female figure of Rodina on a hill near Volgograd (formerly Stalingrad). The site and sculpture are imbued with historical symbolism. The hill is a tumulus, believed to be the burial mound of Khan Mamai, the commander of the Golden Horde defeated by the Russian duke Dmitrii Donskoi in the 1380s. The hill also witnessed the battle of Stalingrad which marked a turning point in the Second World War when, in spring 1943, German troops were forced to retreat from Soviet territory. Against this historical memory the revival of the traditional concept of 'motherland' in its material manifestation of a protective woman is of utmost symbolic significance. The point was not missed on Vladimir Putin who, during his presidential election campaign in February 2000, visited the Volgograd war memorial. The event was well publicised by the state-controlled Russian media.

During the Soviet era it was difficult to judge to what extent socialist ideology had infused traditional social and cultural life both of Russians and non-Russians. Certainly in popular folk art there was evidence of the perpetuation of custom and belief, among them appreciation of Mother Russia (Karlsson, 1999). A reminder of the mother cult in Soviet Russia is preserved in the *matrioshka* dolls which fit one inside the other; the doll was designed in the late 1890s by the Russian artist Sergei Vasil'evitch Maliutin (1859–1937). According to Hubbs (1988): 'Like the ancient Great Mother Goddess, the Matrioshka spills all creation out of her body; like the protective and nurturing individual mother, she gathers her children "under her skirts", where they must find identity through nature's cyclical rhythms of confinement and release' (237).

After the demise of Leninist ideology and the dissolution of the Soviet state, Russia was revived as a political concept, together with traditional Russianness. Mother Russia, concealed beneath a thin layer of socialist ideology, was unveiled and reinstated. This shift was not occasioned by the collapse of Soviet society but rather by the crises which the collapse engendered. Indeed, Russia today is a country of permanent crisis, whether in politics, economics or in society itself. Instability, corruption and poverty have become a way of life for many, and the revival of traditional Russianness is a phenomenon perhaps best explained in terms of a reaction to the present chaos. Various factors contribute to the chaos in present-day Russia where people are under constant pressure to improvise for their physical and psychological survival. These factors include a lack of community feeling, a lack of stability, and a lack of cultural and political orientation.

Lack of community feeling stems from the movement in post-Soviet times towards materialism and egocentricity (in contrast to the Soviet period when community took precedence over the individual). There is growing mistrust on the part of the individual towards society, political authority and state bureaucracy. The negative attitude is furthered by government inability to control socioeconomic change. Capitalism at its most crass is to be found in modern Russia where the newly rich transfer money abroad and dash all hope of general economic prosperity. As gross national product collapses, attempts at reform are stifled; at the same time Russian criminal organisations control more than 80% of the financial markets and their members are influential in government.

Lack of social stability became apparent after the collapse of the Russian currency in late summer 1998. Wages remain unpaid and consumers have no access to goods. Most Russians rely on improvisation to get by and, as a result, the black market flourishes. Since money is rare, an exchange economy has developed; goods and services are swapped for other goods and services. Poverty abounds and the socioeconomic status of Russia is that of a developing country. Revenue from taxation, on which the exchequer depends, corresponds to that of a small country such as Finland. There are no financial resources for social reforms, and the health service, for instance, can barely cope with the increasing incidence of diseases such as diphtheria and tuberculosis. It is against this background of decline and deprivation that fantasies of salvation and political myth-making have achieved their popularity.

Lack of cultural orientation is a result of the swamping of Russian society with western goods and ideas. Most visible are the luxury items in shops and department stores accessible only to a small section of the population. Russian culture has been penetrated by Western popular entertainment such as music, films and video games or publications. Western layout dominates newspapers and journals, while monolingual Russian or English–Russian fashion magazines or books are produced by Russian publishers. The language itself is exposed to an enlarging core of English loan-words. While some Russians welcome the fresh influences on indigenous culture, others see in them a threat to traditional values and, in searching for cultural identity, turn to a Russian past.

Finally, lack of political orientation is a consequence of the relinquishing of Soviet grip on politics in eastern Europe and of the dissolution of the Warsaw Pact. At this point Russia was effectively downgraded from superpower to ordinary nuclear power. The Soviet Union's global political influence ceased and was not replaced by any other grand strategy. Moreover, the first war the Russian army waged against the rebel republic of Chechnya (1995–96) was unsuccessful and the reputation of the once glorified armed forces fell to a record low. In the second war with the Chechens (starting September 1999), the Russian army partly regained its reputation which was tarnished, however, by the wholesale destruction of residential areas and by allegations of human rights violations. Furthermore, Russia has seen NATO and the European Union expanding to the east. Russia, with a fragile, incipient democracy, is an unreliable partner and cannot participate in this expansion. In Asia, Russia's influence has weakened since communist China restructured the economy on western, market-orientated principles. Western investors find in China what is missing in Russia; political stability to safeguard their investments.

The clash of political wills in Russia – right versus left, moderate versus reformer – has resulted in stalemate. Accordingly, in the face of societal and economic uncertainties it is not surprising that Russians have turned to their past. Figures such as Peter the Great and Catherine the Great are enjoying an unprecedented renaissance in the Russian cultural consciousness, with the result that Vladimir Putin was able to tap into this spirit of a more glorious past and present the military campaign in Chechnya as the defence of Russia and the Russians against the terrorism of Muslim fundamentalists. Putin's victorious presidential campaign testifies to the appeal of the new leader to the majority of Russians and non-Russians.

Identity Change and Language

The radicalism of the sociopolitical changes in the early 1990s produced far-reaching effects on the status and structures of the Russian language. No other world language has experienced such dramatic changes in such a short time as has Russian. For the first time in its history the Russian-speaking population is splitting into a dominant majority, as in Russia, and numerous minorities, as in former Soviet and now independent territories such as Estonia, Ukraine or Georgia. From early eastern Slavic statehood (Kiev) in the Middle Ages until 1991, Russians lived within the borders of a Russian-controlled state. After the dissolution of the Soviet empire, more than 20 million people of Russian descent have lived outside Russia as minorities in foreign countries (Kolstoe, 1995). Here, the status of Russian is that of secondary language. The only former Soviet republic in which Russian, based on the result of a referendum, has been re-assigned its former role as official language is Belarus (the former Belorussian SSR) where since 1995 it has functioned – as in the Soviet era – alongside Belorussian in state administration. Secondary language status is one which Russian has never previously experienced, except as mother tongue among emigrants in western Europe and overseas.

The former role of Russian as 'pan-union language' (Russian *vsesojuznyi yazyk*) in the Soviet era changed into that of state language (Russian *gosudarstvennyi yazyk*), a function inadmissible in Soviet ideology. In reality, Russian has operated as state language since the ninth century (Vernadskii, 1996: 266f). In the Soviet era the autocratic status of Russian was never factually challenged but merely ideologically camouflaged. However, the status of the language in the new Russia has been challenged by the demands of local administration in the non-Russian republics of the Russian Federation. In addition, there are those in Russia who have preserved their local culture and who call for greater autonomy. This is true for the Tatars in Tatarstan, for the Kalmyks in the Kalmyk republic (Khalm-Tangsh), for the Yakuts in central Siberia (in Sakha, the former Yakut republic), and for other nations. In these areas of Russia, the former monopoly of Russian in administration and education has been discarded; Russian exists alongside the local, non-Russian language. Indeed, it is a novelty to speak about different official languages inside Russia (Neroznak, 1995). As a consequence, the increased prestige of the local, non-Russian languages and the broadening of their social functions exerts considerable pressure for modernisation on their linguistic structures. New technical terms have to be created to meet the needs of language in a democratic society, particularly with regard to parliament, administration and an education system in which the medium of instruction is the local language.

Despite a strong drive for the cultural and sociopolitical emancipation of local languages, Russian dominates in several non-Russian republics, especially where there is a majority of Russians. An example is Karelia, the northernmost republic in European Russia. The Karelians, the titular nationality of the territory, are a minority accounting for only 10.8% of a population in which Russians form the majority with 73.7%. Other ethnic groups are Belorussians (6.7%), Ukrainians (3.1%), Finns (2.9%) and Vepsians (0.6%). Russian dominates not only in public life but also in private (Khairov, 1997).

Just as local languages are modernising so, too, is Russian. This is happening in random, piecemeal fashion. In the absence of a unified programme for cultural development, and as a result of conflicting and often controversial proposals, the organised language planning to which Russian was subject in the Soviet era has virtually disintegrated. As a result there is a stream of lexical innovations (new compound words, English loan-words, hybrid elements of English–Russian coinage and new abbreviations) flowing into everyday language, in particular from the media (Zemskaia, 1996). Borrowings from western languages, above all English, are now acceptable and, indeed, appreciated following the re-evaluation of western linguistic influence which took place in the post-Soviet era: 'The resultant westernised image is no longer negative, but both fashionable and prestigious' (Ryazanova-Clarke and Wade, 1999: 137). A broad range of new lexical items has entered Russian, for example, *yappi* 'yuppie', *kliring* 'clearing', *lizing* 'leasing', *server* 'server' (in information technology), *baikshou* 'bike-show' and *imidzh* 'image' (Timofeeva, 1995). It has been claimed that the widening in this way of Russian's functional range has contributed to a weakening of traditional stylistic norms (Babenko, 1999: 159f). Spoken Russian is having a marked influence on written style and, while in Soviet times public speeches were imbued with ideological terminology, modern 'politician speak' is spontaneous and draws on colloquial Russian.

Changes have affected not only the style of the standard language or its lexical structures but also syntax and word formation. For instance, in the later decades of the Soviet era, it was the norm to place the qualifier noun in the genitive after the item qualified (according to the principle *rectum-regens*). Probably under the influence of modern English, the qualifier – according to the principle *regens-rectum* – now often precedes the item qualified (Ryazanova-Clarke and Wade, 1999: 281f). An example is the recent loan-word *ofis-menedzher* 'office manager'. Furthermore, prefix frequency has increased. Among the most widely used is *anti-* (as in *anti-marksizm* 'antimarxism'). This prefix stands symbolically for the rejection of Soviet ideological constraints (Ferm, 1994: 85). Its high frequency in modern Russian is indicative of the controversy engendered by national debate about the reconstruction of Russian society.

A fundamental aspect of the modernisation of Russian is the reshuffling of political nomenclature. For the second time in the 20th century both Russians and non-Russians saw radical change in the names of cities, streets, monuments, republics and institutions. In the post-revolutionary Soviet state, the majority of the older Tsarist nomenclature was abolished and replaced by verbal icons of Marxist-Leninist ideology. Now the Soviet tradition has itself been abandoned. The most recent namings partly recall pre-Soviet tradition (as in the reinstatement of historical names for Russian cities) and partly explore neologisms (as in the naming of new offices). Naming is as chaotic as linguistic modernisation itself. An example is the change of the name Leningrad. The historical name St Petersburg was reinstated in 1991 for the city which for decades had carried the name of the icon of the communist movement, Lenin. It is noteworthy that the city changed its name but not the province which is still called *Leningradskaia oblast* 'Leningrad Province'. Leningrad has also been preserved in certain compounds, for instance *Leningradskii vokzal* (Leningrad Station) and *Leningradskoe shossé* (Leningrad Highway) in Moscow.

Russian as the most widely used tool of communication in Russia is beginning to deviate more and more from the language used among Russian-speaking minorities outside Russia. In states bordering Russia – except in Belarus – Russian enjoys no sociopolitical rights: it not taught in schools; it is rarely used in written communication and it remains a minority language confined to the homes and private circles of the Russian diaspora. The Russian language abroad is moving towards the state of a 'roofless vernacular', of a spoken variety of language lacking the 'roof' of a standard language. This term was used by Kloss (1978: 70ff) to describe the situation of German among speakers in the scattered settlements of eastern Europe and overseas.

History in Reverse

The relationship between soil and soul in modern symbolic Russianness draws as much on tradition as on intimacy. Mother Russia has preserved her soul through Tsarist and Soviet times with a tenacity akin to that of the Russian language itself. Of course, this has shown itself under differing sociocultural conditions in various symbolic forms. The manifestations of this archetypal symbol are a result mainly of the multiplicity of sources which have created the tradition (Haarmann, 2000).

Cultural history favours an understanding of Mother Russia as an idea which emerged through intercultural relations. When Slavic tribes settled the Russian plain they made contact with non-Slavs, in particular with Finno-Ugrians. The beliefs of these people, with their respect for mother-spirits and veneration of the earth-mother (Ajkhenvald *et al.*, 1989), suited the Slavs whose own faith in divine femaleness and earth-bound divinity merged with those of their neighbours. Later the idea of Mother Russia, particularly from the 18th century onwards, became increasingly a symbol of Russian nationalism. The idea of the earth-mother, preserved among non-Russians in the empire, came into conflict with Mother Russia as the tool of power politics. Apart from its popularity among ordinary Russians, the concept of Mother Russia was manipulated by the ruling elite of imperial Russia as a vehicle for assimilation of non-Russians with Russians.

A significant change occurred, though, in 1991 when many non-Russians chose to abandon Mother Russia in favour of separation from the former Soviet Union. For Estonians, Latvians, Lithuanians, Belorussians, Ukrainians, Moldavians, Grusinians, Armenians, Azeri, Kazakhs, Uzbeks, Turkmens, Kirghiz and Tadzhiks, the idea of Mother Russia had become obsolete, imbued as it was with colonialism. All the former non-Russian Soviet republics became sovereign states and, even among the peoples of Russia (i.e. in Russia itself), the attitude towards Mother Russia became increasingly problematic. Chechnya is a case in point. For Chechens in the rebel Caucasus republic Mother Russia is an enemy vision, a disguise of covert colonialism. From the first build-up of Russian troops along the Chechen border in December 1994 to the withdrawal of troops from Grozny in August 1996, the Chechen rebels demonstrated their reluctance to embrace – or be embraced by – Mother Russia. This point was seemingly lost on the Russian leadership; even during the second war in Chechnya Russian leaders were determined to inflict the law of Mother Russia on those non-Russians unwilling to acknowledge her authority.

Seemingly, history is reversing itself. Increasing numbers of non-Russians who have experienced the negative effects of a once supportive idea, that of Mother Russia, are critical of the 'benefits' of russification. The soul of Mother Russia, powerful and intimate, may have been revitalised among Russians but it has removed itself from non-Russians at a time of particular crisis and need. Russian nationalism is no answer to legitimate claims for cultural autonomy among the non-Russian peoples of Russia. Arguably, resistance is most intense on the peripheries of modern Russia, in the northern Caucasus, in southern Siberia and also the far north (Slezkine, 1994). There, despite russification, local identity has strengthened among those who retain a grasp on traditional culture and language. It is among these non-Russians (Samoyeds, Tungus and Palaeoasiatic peoples) where traditional consciousness is growing and where community life is organised without help or interference from Russians. According to Fedorov: 'There is no doubt that the culture of the indigenous peoples of the north, particularly their ecological culture, is more complete and organic than the culture of the migrant population [i.e. the Russians] because it reflects a centuries-old homeostasis between man and northern nature' (1998: 38).

Mother Russia is a symbolic marker of Russianness which has proved remarkably flexible and adaptable in the light of differing cultural conditions. It has served the multicultural and multilingual society of traditional Russia and has retained its value even during Soviet rule.

However, for constructing the future identity of modern Russia, it is not sufficient to cling to nationalistic (i.e. Russian) allures or to distortions of the Mother Russia mentality. The army has reinstated Russian autocratic hegemony in Chechnya, but this is woefully incapable of creating trust between Russians and non-Russians. Community life in Russia must modernise; the country must promote reliable strategies of multicultural cooperation to render Mother Russia attractive for non-Russians on her soil. Will Mother Russia prove sufficiently flexible to cope with these challenges?

References

Ajkhenvald, A., Helimski, E. and Petrukhin, V. (1989) On earliest Finno-Ugrian mythologic beliefs: Comparative and historical considerations for reconstruction. In M. Hoppál and J. Pentäikinen (eds) *Uralic Mythology and Folklore* (pp. 155–9). Budapest: Ethnographic Institute of the Hungarian Academy of Sciences; Helsinki: Finnish Literature Society.

Arutiunian, Y.V. (1992) *Russkie. Etno-sotsiologicheskie ocherki*. Moscow: Nauka.

Babenko, N.S. (1999) Die Sprachkultur in Russland vom 18. bis zum 20. Jahrhundert. In J. Scharnhorst (ed.) *Sprachkultur und Sprachgeschichte. Herausbildung und Forderung von Sprachbewusstsein und wissenschaftlicher Sprachpflege in Europa*. Frankfurt/Berlin/New York: Peter Lang.

Danilova, L.V. (1994) *Sel'skaia obshchina v drevnevekovoi Rusi*. Moscow: Nauka.

Fedorov, Y.M. (1998) Kul'turnaia integratsiia. In *Dialog* 8, 38.

Ferm, L. (1994) *Osobennosti razvitiia russkoi leksiki v noveishii period (na materiale gazet)*. Uppsala: Acta Universitatis Upsaliensis, Studia Slavica Upsaliensia 33.

Goscilo, H. (1995) The gendered trinity of Russian cultural rhetoric today – or the glyph of the h[i]eroine. In N. Condee (ed.) *Soviet Hieroglyphics: Visual Culture in Late 20ᵗʰ Century Russia* (pp. 68–92). Bloomington: Indiana University Press.

Haarmann, H. (1995) Multilingualism and ideology: The historical experiment of Soviet language politics. *European Journal of Intercultural Studies* 5, 6–17.

Haarmann, H. (2002) The soul of Mother Russia. Russian symbols and non-Russian cultural identity. *ReVision* (forthcoming).

Hellberg-Hirn, E. (1998) *Soil and Soul: The Symbolic World of Russianness*. Aldershot/Brookfield/Singapore/Sydney: Ashgate.

Hubbs, J. (1988) *Mother Russia: The Feminine Myth in Russian culture*. Bloomington: Indiana University Press.

Karlsson, K.-G. (1999) *Historia som vapen. Historiebruk och Sovjetunionens upplösning 1985–1995*. Stockholm: Natur och Kultur.

Kelly, C. (1998) Popular culture. In N. Rzhevsky (ed.) *The Cambridge Companion to Modern Russian Culture*. Cambridge/New York: Cambridge University Press.

Khairov, Ch. (1997) The functional distribution of the languages of Karelia (Russia). A functional approach to language vitality. *Bulletin de Geolinguistique/Geolinguistic Newsletter* 6, 1–2.

Kloss, H. (1978) *Die Entwicklung neuer germanischer Kultursprachen seit 1800*. Düsseldorf: Wissenschaftliche Buchgesellschaft.

Kolstoe, P. (1995) *Russians in the Former Soviet Republics*. London: Hurst & Co.

Lewis, E.G. (1972) *Multilingualism in the Soviet Union: Aspects of Language Policy and its Implementation*. The Hague/Paris: Mouton.

Likhachev, D. (1991) *Reflections on Russia*. Boulder: Westview Press.

Neroznak, V.P. (ed.) (1995) *Gosudarstvennye yazyki v Rossiiskoi Federatsii. Entsiklopedicheskii slovar'-spravochnik*. Moscow: Nauka.

Ryazanova-Clarke, L. and Wade, T. (1999) *The Russian Language Today*. London/ New York: Routledge.

Slezkine, Y. (1994) *Arctic Mirrors: Russia and the Small Peoples of the North*. Ithaca/ London: Cornell University Press.

Timofeeva, G.G. (1995) *Novye angliiskie zaimstvovaniia v russkom yazyke*. St Petersburg: Yuna.

Tismaneanu, V. (1998) *Fantasies of Salvation: Democracy, Nationalism and Myth in post-communist Europe*. Princeton, NJ: Princeton University Press.

Vernadskii, G.V. (1996) *Istoriia Rossii: Kievskaia Rus'*. Tver': LEAN; Moscow: AGRAF.

Zemskaia, E.A. (1996) Aktivnye protsessy sovremennogo slovoproizvodstva. In E.A. Zemskaia (ed.) *Russkii yazyk kontsa XX stoletiia* (90–141). Moscow.

Chapter 6

Transformation of the State in Western Europe: Regionalism in Catalonia and Northern Italy

BRENDAN MURPHY, CRISTINA DIAZ-VARELA, SALVATORE
COLUCCELLO

Resurgence of conflict between state and nation has characterised
political development in Europe over the last two decades. The collapse
of communism in Eastern Europe led to the disintegration of despotically
created states and to subsequent tension between ethnic groups seeking
to assert identity in the newly formed countries. In Western Europe, too,
resolution of the state-nation problem is embedded in new political
pluralism which, together with establishment of supra-national
institutions, supposedly signals crisis for the nation-state and possibly
its eventual demise.

European economic and political integration has acted as a major spur
to regional nationalism in Western Europe. Regions whose populations
have an identity distinct from their respective nation-states see, as
national sovereignty changes, an opportunity for increased regional
governance and, ultimately, a Europe of the Regions. In the European
Union greater levels of autonomy, even secession, can be contemplated
in politics and economics, with supra-national institutions – the single
market, structural funds, the Council of Ministers and the Committee of
the Regions – providing a degree of safety in converting regionalist
aspirations into new geopolitical realities. Furthermore, because regionalism is multidimensional, taking widely varying political, territorial and
functional forms and reflecting a diverse mix of identities (socio-
economic, religious, cultural, linguistic, etc.), it can be argued that, at
the level of governance, there is room for solutions to satisfy regional
aspirations in each particular case. This is particularly so in the

73

developing European polity in which governance is increasingly multilayered and in which a regional tier is seen as essential to economic performance, redistributive policies and political representation.

In Italy and Spain the central state is under pressure to transform itself from both supra-national and sub-national levels. Satisfaction of regionalist demands was the major issue facing architects of the post-Franco democratic polity in Spain, and the last two decades have seen the autonomous communities and regional elections acquire increasing significance in Spanish political life. In Italy, since the political crisis of the early 1990s, the Northern League has emerged as a major advocate of radical overhaul of state institutions through adoption of a federal system. The Northern League has also toyed with the notion of secession of Padania[1] from the Italian state.

It is clear, however, that the European dimension is only one of a number of factors that have motivated regionalism since the Second World War. Other major factors, particularly in the cases of Spain and Italy, have been:

- crisis or collapse of traditionally weak states;
- decline of centrally controlled networks of patronage and clientelism;
- economic success in states with wide economic disparities – both Catalonia and Padania see for themselves a key role in the economic rebirth of southern Europe, and the main regionalist parties in each make great play of their representation of the interests of a vibrant indigenous business class;
- the collapse of communism and the subsequent legitimisation of the political left. In Italy this weakened the bipolar hegemony which kept the communists out of power and made political space for the Northern League;
- a historic sense of ethnic difference. Catalonia is a prima-facie case of a region whose regional identity rests on language, culture, history and institutions distinct from the central state.

The following considers Padania and Catalonia in the changing political culture of Italy, Spain and the EU. It will be argued that while significant differences exist between each region – particularly in terms of the ethnolinguistic foundations of regional sentiment – broad similarities can be isolated both in the roots of, and in the search for, new political identity. Catalonia and northern Italian regions such as Piedmont and Lombardy are among those Mediterranean areas that have been quickest to modernise,[2] and to a certain extent they therefore have more in common with northern than southern Europe. This is largely because these areas underwent successful transition from non-industrial to industrial societies during the nineteenth century, with strongly indigenous capital formation, concentration of national industrial society in their borders, and growth of powerful autochthonous mercantile classes and banking sectors. But in both Spain and Italy modern capitalism and industrialism were enclave phenomena – that is, while these privileged regions were undergoing their transition to modernity, most other parts remained backward, predominantly agricultural and traditional (Giner, 1997). Thus, as explained in more detail below, Padanian and Catalan regionalisms offer themselves as forces for a 'europeanist' modernisation in countries that continue to suffer the supposed legacy of southern European backwardness – late industrialisation occurring in states which are highly interventionist yet administratively weak and which therefore resort to an ultimately destructive clientelism, and which are characterised by low levels of political institutionalisation (Sapelli, 1995: 20).

Regions, Regionalism and Sub-national Politics

The difficulties of defining region are well-documented (Keating, 1998: 18). A region is a sub-national territorial unit but the political, economic, geographical and institutional forms regions may take in European societies are subject to variation. The territory which is the object of regionalist consciousness may be contested, regional borders may bridge more than one national boundary, regions may be metropolitan or provincial or widely differing in size. Furthermore, sub-national political cultures are not necessarily tied to regions but may be local or municipal, as in Italy.

In terms of institutional status regions may simply be a decentralised administrative agency of the central state. This was largely the case in the United Kingdom where Scotland, Wales – before creation of separate parliaments – and Northern Ireland were administered essentially from Whitehall, with respective ministers being members of a cabinet in a central government. In contrast are federations such as Germany, Austria and Belgium where regional parliaments enjoy powers and functions exercised centrally in other European nations. The Spanish and Italian regional systems can be seen as intermediate cases in which autonomy has resulted in some transfer of central power to regional parliaments, but with initially limited fiscal responsibility. In Spain, the transfer of power from the centre is now well advanced and regions enjoy different degrees of autonomy. All 17 autonomous communities are responsible for education, public works, communication and transport, environment, regional development and tourism, but seven of the regions, including Catalonia, have greater powers which cover also public health, social security, local administration and policing (Amodia, 1998: 35).

In Europe the region has undergone substantial change as perceptions of territoriality have shifted in response to a changing political economy; there is no uniform model of geopolitical organisation but a number of interacting forms and levels. This is particularly so in Europe where internationalisation of political and economic institutions is regulated in a triangle of governance between supra-national, national and sub-national institutions.

After the Second World War, Keynesian macroeconomic management made regions the foci for economic development in overall national demand management, with reduction of economic disparities to be achieved through diversion of investment to underprivileged regions. The aim was to balance economic development between regions by removing inflationary pressures from prosperous areas while at the same time improving resources and stimulating demand and production in peripheral regions. In this way social cohesion could be improved, budgetary pressures eased on central government, and the regions reintegrated into the national political economy. The public agencies set up in Italy to deal with the 'mezzogiorno' question are an example of these efforts at regional equalisation.

The crisis of Keynesianism and the growth of neoliberalism through the 1980s produced a situation in which national governments tended to favour prosperous regions. International capital mobility, and EU competition law in particular, seriously limit the power of governments to affect investment decisions on behalf of underdeveloped regions. However, far from undermining regional nationalisms, international-isation has tended rather to strengthen them, albeit with a different set of aspirations, priorities and potentials. Globalised markets and com-munications, and international specialisation and division of labour, have brought about the need for more diversified and flexible production to cope with international demand. In such a political economy, regional governments are well placed to coordinate the institutional, political, social and cultural input required for economic advancement through attracting international investment. The needs of a regional economy are felt to be more accurately assessed at sub-national level, while local information can be readily applied to mobilise key agents in the economy (Hirst and Thompson, 1996: 147).

Obviously, such a scenario may tend to exacerbate rather than reduce regional disparities, as regions must not only compete with each other for international influence but also negotiate transfer of power from central government – power which itself is increasingly constrained by the international political economy.

The problems of defining region lead to similar difficulties with regionalism. However, it is clear that sub-national territorial consciousness means different things to different people, not just in Europe but elsewhere. Regional identities are normally multidimensional and include issues of socio-economic structure, religion, ethnicity and ideology. The distinguishing feature in regional nationalism, however, is that these issues are accompanied by a notion of sub-national territoriality which becomes the focus for political activity (Lane and Ersson, 1987).

West European regionalism is highly varied with regard to cause, ideological position and demands. Nonetheless, regionalism is commonly associated with claims for collective equality that are rooted in grievances over territory, language, culture and economic disadvantage. Williams (1997) identifies three main issues which sustain most forms of regionalism:

(1) promotion and protection of a unique language and culture;
(2) enhanced economic autonomy to further industrial modernisation or to reverse regional industrial decline;
(3) more democratic forms of political representation.

But, as stated above, political systems which seek to resolve such issues and, at the same time, equalise economic disparities may, given internationalisation and economic liberalisation, cause underprivileged regions to fall further behind.

In Spain, the reduction of regional inequalities was a major factor in creating the state of the autonomies (Heywood, 1995: 152). Nevertheless, wide regional disparities remain which have led to regionalisms that differ through their relationship with central administration. While the 'decentralist' Catalan regionalists continue to seek ever greater control over their own affairs, poorer regions such as Andalusia and Extremadura have formed a more 'integrative' and pro-centralist identity as they seek to participate more fully in national life. The competitive advantage of these poorer regions remains dependent to a large extent on redistribution administered through an interterritorial compensation fund coordinated from Madrid with the aim of equalising regional disparities. However, both Andalusia and Extremadura have been cautious over moves towards greater fiscal autonomy in the 1990s. A similar set of centre-periphery relations pertains in Italy, with a significant level of northern opposition to a central administration that coordinates national redistribution which is felt to be unfairly weighted in favour of the economically backward south.

An important element in the development of West European regionalism has been consolidation and renewal of democracy. In both Spain and Germany the establishment of democracy was closely linked to the creation and strengthening of a sub-national tier of government; similarly Scotland and Wales now espouse some form of self-determination as vital to renewal of what are perceived to be outmoded central political structures in the United Kingdom. In this way weak and decayed forms of governance can be transformed through regionalisation of national politics. Of course, party politics and political personalities play a key role in such a process – in Spain a regional political elite is emerging and interacting in significant ways with national politics. The present prime minister, José María Aznar, became leader of the ruling Popular Party after success as head of the regional government of Castilla y León. Other regional presidents such as Manuel Fraga (Galicia) and Manuel Chaves (Andalusia) enjoy a high profile. Regional presidents have also begun to undertake official visits abroad, causing confusion and controversy with the central authorities over the status of foreign policy in the Spanish constitution (García, 1995: 127).

As indicated, European integration has led to a resurgence of regional politics such that the traditional territorial political identity – the nation-state – is challenged by both supra-national and sub-national institutions. A centre-periphery model is no longer sufficient to account for European regional politics. An essentially triangular relationship is forming between European, national and regional institutions of governance in a political order of dispersed authority and shared sovereignty. As such institutions, responsibilities and memberships overlap and it remains to be seen how the diverse nationalisms and secessionist aspirations of the regions will be incorporated into the developing European polity (Keating, 1998: 25).

While regions are set to play an increasingly important role in European governance, it is unlikely to mean a decline of central administrations, despite apocalyptic claims by the more excitable eurosceptics. As already noted, there is no uniform model of sub-national territorial organisation in EU member states which, in turn, creates a mismatch between the status of the region at supra-national and national levels. Hence, while the future importance of regions in European governance seems assured, the European Union, driven primarily by economics, is likely further to diversify regional administration and politics. In a framework of multifarious and interrelated institutions – nation-states, the EU itself, regions, metropolitan areas, corporations, public lobbies, etc. – competition and cooperation over resource allocation (economic and political) is increasingly operating across traditional geopolitical boundaries. Europe is developing a 'geography of common interests' in which the economic needs of regions such as Lombardy and Catalonia have more in common with each other than with, for instance, Campania and Extremadura. Thus, for regions, political claims can no longer be satisfied exclusively through renewal of single-state relations between centre and periphery.

Sub-national politics in modern Spain and Italy can be explained by two major socio-economic and historical-political determinants. First, both are countries with wide disparities between richer and poorer areas, with less privileged regions relying on central administration for support while richer regions argue for increasing freedom to pursue indigenous economic development. The second, related, factor is that industrial and financial power in both Spain and Italy is located outside the political and administrative capitals, in regions with strong sub-national territoriality – in Barcelona and Bilbao, and in Turin and Milan. These socio-economic factors have become increasingly important in the redefinition of Spanish and Italian national politics since the early 1990s.

However, the roots of regional identity are very different in Catalonia and Padania and in the sub-national fabric of Spain and Italy generally. The sub-national political culture of Spain has traditionally been strongly linked to regions. The unification, or reconquest, of Spain brought together independent Christian kingdoms, many of which form the basis for the autonomous communities of the modern Spanish state. Catalonia itself enjoyed seven centuries of independence, building a Mediterranean empire, until unification with the crown of Aragón. Institutionally, sub-national government in Spain until the 1930s was predominantly provincial and municipal, particularly following the eighteenth-century Bourbon reforms. Emergence of regional politics in the nineteenth century was closely associated with attempts, frequently unsuccessful, at social, political, economic and institutional modernisation. It was not until the 1978 constitution that the aspirations of the 'historic' regions for increased self-determination were met, and since 1980 there has been considerable transfer of power from the centre to the autonomous regional governments.

By contrast, Italian sub-national political culture is local and municipal, reflecting in large degree the organisation of Italian political life from medieval times around the city-states. After 1945, despite strong pressure from the periphery for regional government – from Sicily, Sardinia, Trentino-Alto Adige and Friuli Venezia-Giulia – in more central areas the regional issue was far less deeply felt; there was no deep-rooted regional identification in the populations of most parts of Italy. While administrative reorganisation in the 1970s saw the creation of regional governments, no Italian regions (other than the Islands) expressed the type of nationalism, based on distinct language, culture and history, found in Catalonia, the Basque country, Galicia and, to a lesser extent, Valencia and Navarre (Levy, 1996).

Basic territorial cleavage in modern Italy is the product of specific historical and economic circumstances which have produced a strong north-south divide. The north of Italy, where the major industrial and financial areas are located, enjoys levels of economic advancement comparable with any in Western Europe – for example, through the 1980s, Lombardy (Italy's richest region) had the highest rate of growth of any European region at 8% of GDP per annum. For the south, an obvious difficulty is geographical remoteness from major national and continental centres of population and production. Germany and Austria are only three hours or so from north-east Italy but a similar journey time links Palermo and Messina, or Bari and Tirana. The Italian south also suffers difficult terrain and poor climate as well as a legacy of centuries of absentee landlords and stunted capital development. Its service sector, plus transport and communications, are also weak. A southern entrepreneur spends twice the amount required by a northern counterpart to export goods to Europe. The alternative is to rely on the deficient southern internal market or on other, poorer, overseas destinations such as North Africa.

Since the Second World War measures have been implemented to try to reduce the north-south gap. The *cassa per il mezzogiorno* diverted public funds towards commerce, agriculture, industry and infrastructure in the south. Public support for the south was drastically reduced from the end of the 1980s and the area remains economically dependent, albeit less on transfers from the north rather than European regional funding (Zamagni, 1999).

Regionalism and Political Crisis

Crisis in the national state in the 1970s and 1980s saw consolidation of regional politics in Spain and its re-emergence in Italy. Fundamental to the post-Franco transition to democracy was the need to solve the regional issue. This had been one of the major causes of the civil war and had been left to fester during 39 years of Francoist cultural repression and institutional vacuum. Establishment of the state of the autonomies was fundamental to the new Spain and essential to national consensus without which change could not succeed. Initially, the autonomies enjoyed limited competencies but the last 15 years have seen further powers transferred from the centre.

The modern Italian regions were created as the result of administrative reforms undertaken after turmoil in the late 1960s in industry and the universities. The slow pace of social and political reform under the centre-left government from 1963–68 led to popular clamour for a radical overhaul of state institutions. In partial response, the government established a regional tier of administration, relatively weak, but with control over, *inter alia*, health, regional infrastructure and urban planning.

The 1990s brought further political crisis to both countries and, in each case, saw a renegotiation of the party political system with an enhanced role for the regions. In Spain this involved two main factors. First, the Spanish Socialist Party (PSOE, Partido Socialista Obrero Español), in government since 1982, underwent a rapid decline from the early 1990s, primarily as a result of economic policy failures, and the involvement of high-ranking public officials and leading socialist politicians (including government ministers) in corruption scandals. Second, the conservative Popular Party (PP, Partido Popular) failed until 1996 to disassociate itself from its neofrancoist heritage. This prevented a national centre-right alternative to the PSOE uniting the PP and the hegemonic centre-right regionalist parties of Catalonia and the Basque country. The elections of 1993 and 1996 were inconclusive. In the first the PSOE lost its parliamentary majority and was forced to govern with the Catalan nationalists, Convergence and Union (CiU, Convergencia i Unió). In 1996, though, the PP established itself as the biggest party in parliament and, perhaps surprisingly, formed a coalition government with the Basque Nationalist Party (PNV, Partido Nacionalista Vasco) and CiU. Both the 1993 and 1996 elections therefore saw regionalist parties participating in national government and extracting as the price of electoral support transfer of power from the centre.

In 1990s Italy, crisis has meant wholesale reorganisation of the party political system. The so-called historical compromise between the Christian Democrats (DC, Democrazia Cristiana) and the Socialist Party (PSI, Partito Socialista Italiano), which had governed Italy from 1980 to 1992, was shaken by economic crisis and corruption. Investigation revealed the inherent instability of Italy's political system and resulted in the decline of the central role of parliament in political management of the country (Sapelli, 1995: 193). The main Italian parties started to lose votes to the Greens, the Refounded Communists and the Northern League, and the voting system was changed in 1993 with adoption of elements of first-past-the-post. This was an attempt to reduce the political fragmentation that continually frustrated outright electoral success and to limit the political horse-trading in coalition governments. The influence of the Northern League's regionalist demands was illustrated in 1997 when a parliamentary commission presented a draft proposal for further constitutional reforms, to involve an enhanced role for the regions through devolution of major areas of administrative and fiscal power (Keating, 1998: 133).

Principal protagonists in regional politics in Spain and Italy are representatives of Catalonia and Padania. Catalan regionalism is strongly linked both to industrial entrepreneurs and to promotion of interests through disengagement from a corrupt, archaic state as a route to economic advancement and modernisation. Elements of this bourgeois nationalism are also characteristic of the Northern League, although with a more aggressively populist right-wing stance on immigration both from the south of Italy and from countries outside the European Union. Bourgeois regionalism is characteristic of wealthier regions in weak states, and expresses the desire of economically advanced areas to unshackle themselves from inefficient central administrations whose wastefulness drains resources from more productive and industrially modern areas to regions still dominated by tradition, inefficiency and patronage. Such regionalist politics is frequently driven by a 'modernizing regional technocracy, often tied to the public sector management and to the planning profession' (Keating, 1998: 105).

Characteristic of this bourgeois regionalism is protest against what is felt to be weak, corrupt, clientelistic control exercised by central governments in Madrid and Rome. In both Padania and Catalonia there is a perception that in the poorer regions the power brokers fail to exploit the 'horizontal' potential of the region, by promoting interregional networks of political association and economic advancement, and instead use their 'vertical' links with the centre for resource distribution rather than sustainable economic development. Links between regions are weak as they remain subordinated to party machinery that functions along particularistic lines.

For Sapelli (1995), southern European political systems manifest a tension between modern party political institutions and traditional participation in public life. This has been possible in Spain and Italy because capitalism developed after, or perhaps at the same time as, the democratic political class. Politicians found themselves able to intervene in the market since, in the absence of strong and spontaneous upsurges of indigenous capital formation, they were largely responsible for its development. Across society there is widespread private use of public functions and resources and a large element of governance involves division of the spoils by the parties, rather than by general application of laws according to legal and bureaucratic rationality (Sapelli, 1995: 115). Thus the PSOE stronghold in southern Spain was only partially rooted in socialist (or social-democratic) ideology and more in arrangements for distribution of resources to the rural poor through social subsidies, public investments and employment schemes.

In 1993 around 250,000 Spaniards in Andalusia and Extremadura were receiving public money under the Régimen Especial Agrario (REA), which entitled claimants to nine months' unemployment benefit if they could prove they had worked for a minimum of sixty days. Additionally the PSOE instituted a public works scheme, mainly involving infrastructure – the Plan de Empleo Rural (PER) – and permitted days worked on such schemes to be counted towards eligibility for the REA. While centrally funded these projects were under local control in terms of planning and hiring of labour. The mainly socialist mayors of Andalusia and Extremadura emerged to replace landowners as arbiters of local networks of social patronage through a party-controlled system open to fraud and corruption. Despite frequent calls to reform or even abolish a scheme that exacerbated disincentives to work or migrate, the PSOE in 1995 – though in the midst of an annual cycle of fiscal adjustment to reduce budget deficit in preparation for EMU – actually eased eligibility requirements for the REA and increased its entitlements (OECD, 1996: 75). It is unsurprising that, despite the declining fortunes of the PSOE in urban areas, its vote in rural areas rose throughout the 1990s.

Catalan nationalism has historically been founded on a belief that the backward Spanish state could achieve socio-economic, institutional and political modernisation through the supposed virtues of the Catalan bourgeois revolution (Solé-Tura, 1970). More recently – in the 1980s and early 1990s – party patronage operated by the Andalusian-dominated socialist governments that engaged in subsidisation of southern inefficiencies and waste, and the supposed disadvantages to the wealthier northern regions of interregional redistribution, became factors in Catalan arguments for fairer and enhanced fiscal powers for the autonomous communities.

The Northern League espouses a federal, or even secessionist, solution to the perceived problem of the malpractices of central Italian government which drains resources from the prosperous north for redistribution to the underdeveloped south – made possible for many decades by patronage operated by the ruling DC and their political clients in the south. Despite significant transfers of funding arrangements to European institutions, serious imbalances remain in Italian regional redistribution. In 1995 the southern region of Campania received public funds of $2.5 billion, while Veneto, in the north, received only $130 million, having contributed $9 billion. Veneto remains the fourth biggest contributor but is third from bottom in terms of receipts. This disadvantage is the main factor in the growth of a sense of injustice in northern Italy and unites the regions under the Northern League's slogan 'Roma Ladrone!' (Gilbert, 1995).

Indeed, the Northern League has taken upon itself the role of moral conscience of Italian political life, protesting against the *tangentopoli* – illegal financing of major national parties by big businesses in exchange for political favours – and against widespread collusion between central government and organised crime in the south which has been a major beneficiary of public funds channelled to the area.

Ethnolinguistic and Cultural Identities

Although Catalan and Padanian regionalisms both incorporate protest against central clientelism and corruption, this tendency is more prevalent in the case of the Northern League, while in Catalonia protest reinforces extant national identity rooted in historical difference expressed through national language and a coherent culture. It can be argued that the Northern League, in the absence of historical Padanian regional identity, is the result of prosperity which spread through Italy in the 1980s (during the second economic boom) and that a 'regional' basis for anti-centre protest is being invoked to protect northern Italian comparative advantage in the Italian state. For Sapelli (1995: 193) the Northern League espouses bogus regionalist politics to justify lack of national solidarity rooted in simple economic grievance:

> [The Northern League] created a territorially based political and cultural fracture which, not by chance, involved the richer part of the country. This section of society had no desire to give up its recently won well-being when the economic crisis appeared and the distributive conflicts typical of the state's periods of fiscal crisis started.

If nationalism is taken to include, at some level, common language, race, culture or religion – as constituents of the same primordial entity, the nation – it is surely difficult to consider the Northern League as representative of true regionalist identity.

In Catalonia the Catalan language has been a major element both in promoting Catalan unity and in cementing the political and institutional status of Catalan regionalism itself. Catalan is a recognised Romance language spoken by over six million people and has become the focus, since the 1980s, of laws promoting its use in education and public administration in the Catalan Autonomous Community. Thus, while Catalonia has a recognised indigenous language used in well-defined territorial limits and co-official with Castilian Spanish, northern Italy can boast no such linguistic distinctiveness with respect to the centre, nor homogeneity in its borders. In Italy dialects are attached to cities rather than regions, and in Padania there is no standard northern Italian language or dialect that can be used as a reference for expression of regional distinctiveness.

Because of this the Northern League has made great efforts to invoke cultural myths and tokens that can support Padanian identity. The image of Alberto da Giussano, a crusader who led a coalition of northern Italian cities against Frederick Barbarossa, was superimposed on the flag of Lombardy and became the party emblem. History was also used to support myth creation; Pontida, where delegates of the medieval Lombard League took a war oath, became from 1989 the meeting-place for Northern League members. In 1996, the Northern League started publication of *La Padana*, a daily newspaper carrying news (and weather) from northern Italian regions. In the European Parliament Northern League deputies have, significantly, achieved inclusion in the parliamentary group to which Scottish Nationalist MEPs belong; Scotland is a region to which the Northern League looks for inspiration and strategic models (Keating, 1998; Diamanti, 1993).

However, while northern Italy might seem to be an uncertain territorial entity, voting patterns reveal that the territorial limits of Padania are well defined. The Northern League achieves consistent support in the nine regions of Padania, suggesting there is a territorial coherence in voter identification with the party programme. Nevertheless, the regional economies of northern Italy are characterised to a significant degree by small and family businesses, a voting class which largely identifies with the anti-centre protest articulated by the Northern League. It is noteworthy that, before the collapse of communism in Eastern Europe in 1989, this electoral group voted mainly for the governing coalition. The subsequent transfer of political loyalties to the Northern League can be explained in part by the ending of entrepreneurial fear of Soviet expansionism through the Italian Communist Party.

Since its foundation in the early 1980s the Northern League has failed to gain power beyond the local level, notwithstanding brief experience of national coalition government with Berlusconi's Forza Italia and Alleanza Nazionale. Its main victories have been in municipal elections; for instance, in 1993 it gained control of most major cities in the north of Italy, including Milan. By contrast the main Catalan nationalist party, CiU, has controlled the *generalitat* – the autonomous government of the Catalan region – since 1980 and has been a partner in national government since 1993. This has enabled Catalan nationalists to make ever greater claims on national sovereignty, particularly with regard to fiscal autonomy. The strongly devolutionist programme of CiU is thus tempered by working relations with the centre in Spain's mixed regional model, and reflects the oft-repeated claim that the party seeks autonomy and not independence from a state with which its economy is interdependent. Electoral success is reflected in a relatively coherent political programme of europeanist, progressive and conservative social capitalism, and the promotion of Catalan economic, political and cultural interests in Spain.

By contrast the Northern League is prone to programmatic imprecision and populist rhetoric in its search for a wider electoral base. Anti-centre protest is accompanied by virulent attacks on immigrants – initially directed at Southern Italians and more recently towards those from overseas (Diamanti, 1993). Initially pro-federalist, the Northern League now veers between secession, devolution, autonomy and federalism, although its most consistent call is for the creation of a federal Italy, with three 'super-regions' in the north, centre and south. There is ambiguity at the heart of Padanian regionalism to the extent that its political representatives remain undecided about the nature and degree of power being sought.

Perhaps the most significant element in both northern Italian and Catalan regionalism is the international and European orientation of both. Indeed, the Northern League chose as one of its slogans 'further from Rome and closer to Europe' and initially proposed inclusion of Padania in EMU, with the centre and south to be left using the lira. Both see themselves as protagonists in the regeneration of southern European economics and are active in promoting interregional cooperation in Europe. Both look towards the Europe of the Regions as the ultimate guarantor of their regional interests.

Regional politics in the EU is already well established through interregional cooperation and lobbying in the institutions of European governance, and the Treaty of Union provided for creation of the Committee of the Regions (García, 1995: 129). Catalonia and northern Italy are involved, for instance, in cooperative ventures such as the 'Four Motors of Europe' (Catalonia, Baden-Württemberg, Rhone-Alpes and Lombardy) and the West-Mediterranean Euro-Region (Catalonia, Languedoc-Roussillon and Midi-Pyrenees). Both are instances of 'macroregional' partnerships that can bypass national governments in favour of direct EU lobbying for resources.

Both areas look to an enhanced role for the Committee of the Regions to transfer further power to sub-national governments most probably through inclusion of regional, along with national, representatives in the European Parliament. Accordingly, the Northern League argues for a bicameral European Parliament with one house consisting of representatives of regions, irrespective of the constitutional arrangements of its specific community (Sentini, 1993). In this sense Europe would be *de facto* a federation, regardless of the *de jure* status of the European polity, as power would be devolved to the sub-national level by the supra-national level, having previously been transferred by nation-states. It is important to recognise that this would take place in a context of multilateral and interdependent forms of governance. What is envisaged by Catalonia and Padania in the context of a European regional role is a new form of power and potential in which regions mediate between supra-national and national levels, forging new territorial blocs, by virtue of common economic and cultural interests, and increasing the role of the regions in directing policy in the European institutions.

Catalonia and Padania exemplify the diverse nature of regional politics in Europe. Catalonia is a well-established region in terms of historical and cultural identity. This it does not share with Padania and, as indicated, the Northern League is trying to compensate by adopting cultural and mythical tokens of northern Italian identity. Both regionalisms are rooted in bourgeois entrepreneurism and espouse values of modern free-market capitalism. They therefore have strong economic reasons for a fervently europeanist orientation and for radical reform in central states that supposedly act as a brake on their social and economic advancement. However, Catalonia shows no real desire to secede from Spain but is working to achieve as much devolution as possible under the Spanish constitution. Indeed, Catalan nationalism is unlikely to enjoy the political power currently available to it since the CiU leader Jordi Pujol is a major partner in the conservative governing coalition. This is illustrated by the coalition agreement between the PP and CiU (1996) which increased the fiscal power of the autonomous communities in Spain and enhanced regional participation in European issues. The Northern League reflects a greater level of dissatisfaction with the institutional apparatus of the Italian state and therefore fluctuates between calls for outright secession and a new federal Italy. However, it is Europe and the global economy which will ultimately determine regional government in each area. Regions are likely to increase in political status in Europe; sub-national government will play an enhanced role in the coordination of local agencies vital to compete successfully in the international economy for capital investment.

In conclusion, regional identities are subject to change according to specific circumstances. Italy and Spain in the 1990s are both undergoing redefinition of their political systems, involving new identities which incorporate sub-national territorial claims. While there is significant contrast between the two states in the upsurge of regional nationalisms – Catalan and Basque nationalisms are both founded on ethnolinguistic and sociohistorical distinctiveness while the north of Italy cannot truly make any such claim – developments in the European and international political economy have brought the demands of these two regions to the fore. In a context of internationalised trade and communications, together with fiscal rigour and investment-friendly policies that characterise the current phase of European integration, Catalonia and Padania can make convincing claims to be regions vital to the economic future of their respective states. As such, their economic prestige is starting to reap political benefit both at national level, in moves to greater transfer of powers to the regions, and at European level, in the development of a 'Europe of the Regions' and in creation of international cooperation.

These developments could be said to be characteristic of the whole of Western Europe, but it can further be argued that Spain and Italy have reached a particular point in their political development; establishment and consolidation of democracy following authoritarian rule. Clearly, Italy moved towards political pluralism before Spain, but each democracy has similar problems which plague implantation of truly pluralist forms of representation, and regionalism is making a significant contribution to redefinition of the political system in both states. In the 1990s both Spain and Italy reached a crisis when it became apparent that much custom and practice of the pre-democratic sociopolitical structure – chiefly associated with personalistic networks of influence, control and access to resources – had not been eliminated but rather absorbed by the political class in a neoclientelistic *partitocrazia*. Rightly or wrongly, essential to dismantling and restructuring of party and electoral systems in each state is devolution of power to the regions and, at the same time, to the supranational level in European institutions. As Keating (1998: 87–8) puts it:

The new state context facilitates this construction of alternative identities, both by weakening the prestige of the established states, and by providing opportunities for regional leaders to project their regions and themselves in the international and European arenas.

Such a panorama is favourable to Catalonia and Padania as they enjoy comparative advantages vital in the competitive international environment that will inevitably result. Both have the necessary economic infrastructure to take full advantage of the federalist direction of the EU.

Notes

1. Padania is the invented name given to a collective of northern Italian regions which are the territorial foci for the Northern League's efforts to forge a new sub-national political identity in Italy.
2. Modernisation is a complex term. Here it is used to signal the transformation from a traditional agrarian society to an industrial and urban one, with the attendant social, political and cultural changes this entails.

References

Amodia, J. (1998) Politics in contemporary Spain: Establishing and consolidating a new democracy. In T. Lawlor and M. Rigby (eds) *Contemporary Spain: Essays and Texts on Politics, Economics, Education and Employment, and Society*. London: Longman.

Diamanti, I. (1993) *La Lega*. Roma: Donselli.

García, C. (1995) The autonomous communities and external relations. In R. Gillespie, F. Rodrigo and J. Story (eds) *Democratic Spain: Reshaping External Relations in a Changing World*. London: Routledge.

Gilbert, M. (1995) *The Italian Revolution: The End of Politics, Italian Style?* Oxford: Westview Press.

Giner, S. (1997) *Catalonia: The Tradition of Modernity*. Fourth Ramón Pérez de Ayala Lecture, University of Southampton, 24 November.

Heywood, P. (1995) *The Government and Politics of Spain*. London: Macmillan.

Hirst, P. and Thompson, G. (1996) *Globalization in Question: The International Economy and the Possibilities of Governance*. Cambridge: Polity Press.

Keating, M. (1998) *The New Regionalism in Western Europe*. Cheltenham: Edward Elgar.

Lane, J-E. and Ersson, S. (1987) *Politics and Society in Western Europe*. London: Sage.

Levy, C. (1996) *Italian Regionalism*. New York: Berg.

OECD (1996) Spain 1995–1996. Paris: OECD Economic Surveys.
Sapelli, G. (1995) *Southern Europe Since 1945: Tradition and Modernity in Portugal,
   Spain, Italy, Greece and Turkey*. London: Longman.
Sentini, V. (1993) *La Lega: Italia a Pezzi? Verso la Seconda Repubblica*. Bolazno: Raetia.
Solé-Tura, J. (1970) *Catalanismo y Revolución Burguesa*. Madrid: Cuadernos para el
   Diálogo.
Williams, C. (1997) Territory, identity and language. In M. Keating and J. Loughlin
   (eds) *The Political Economy of Regionalism*. London: Frank Cass.
Zamagni, V. (1999) Italy. In M-S. Schulze (ed.) *Western Europe: Economic and Social
   Change since 1945*. London: Longman.

Chapter 7

Fixing National Borders: Language and Loyalty in Nice

SUE WRIGHT

The rapid language shift which took place in Nice after it became part of the French state in 1860, having been ceded by the King of Piedmont-Savoy, Victor-Emmanuel II, to Napoleon III, is remarkable. The realignment from being part of the territory of the House of Savoy to incorporation in the French state was so swift and so complete that it cut Nice from its old links and networks. Because of political events it is not surprising that Italian was replaced by French as the language of public life. However, what is surprising is that the local Italian dialect, Nissart, disappeared from the private domain. As ever, when a group chooses to acquire another idiom, the choice is rooted in politics and in the cultural status of speakers of the new language. It is also related to the personal advantage learners hope to acquire by allying themselves with any prestige and with economic and political benefits enjoyed by that language community. Below I examine some of the forces that caused the language shift and which established a clear line between the Italian- and French-speaking worlds along the political border.

Before 1860, Nice and Savoy shared little common history with Paris, the Franks, the Capetians or even with the French Revolution. Nice is more interesting sociolinguistically than Savoy in that its population was not French-speaking before the annexation but underwent a shift to French in a short space of time. This phenomenon cannot be explained as language choice based on a revival of previous attachments, loyalties and common development, because the history of Nice, with links more to the east than to the west, is separate from that of its western neighbour. A résumé of the history of Nice and its hinterland will show that reasons for the rapidity of the language shift will have to be sought elsewhere. They cannot be seen as the result of nationalist irredentism or the return to a shared past.

France the Aggressor

The first inhabitants to whom one can give a name were the Ligurians (d'Hombres, 1877). The town of Nice was founded by the Greeks and reputedly named in honour of their victory over the Ligurians. Subsequently the area fell under Roman domination and was the first and the most profoundly romanised part of present-day France. With the fall of Rome, Nice was attacked by Visigoths, Hérules, Burgundians, Franks and Lombards. However, the most persistent enemies of the post-Roman era were the Saracens, and Nice joined other Ligurian towns to fight them. Nice and Savoy became – like most of Europe – part of Charlemagne's empire. When this broke up in 843, the area eventually became independent and was given to Charles Martel's son-in-law, Boson. When Boson's line died out, the counts of Barcelona took Nice and its hinterland and ruled from 1109 to 1245, whereupon the House of Anjou ruled for over a century. The area prospered on account of trading links but internecine wrangles ruptured the political order and Nice asked to be taken into the protection of the House of Savoy. From 1388–1860 Nice and Savoy were part of greater Piedmont-Savoy and were ruled from Turin. The only exception was during the French revolutionary wars when Nice – again like most of continental Europe – fell under French rule. Given the House of Savoy's alliances during these five centuries, France was often the enemy and aggressor. There were no evident political reasons why Nice or its surrounding area should be or become French-speaking at the time of Italian unification.

Unification had been brought about partly through support from Napoleon III for Victor-Emmanuel, King of Piedmont-Savoy, in his bid to unify Italy and to drive the Habsburgs from the peninsula. In recognition of military and political backing, Nice and its hinterland were to be ceded to France to give Napoleon III the frontier along the Alps that had always been considered desirable for national defence. The deal was struck in a secret treaty at Plombières in 1858 which would be ratified, if the military campaign were successful, by consulting the Niçois (or at least the adult males listed on the suffrage censitaire) in a referendum. Following victories at Magenta and Solferino, which saw the Austrians retaining just Venice and the surrounding area, the French expected to conclude their deal. However, under pressure from the Italian party in Nice, Victor-Emmanuel tried to retain the town and to give up Savoy alone (Compan, 1989). Napoleon III pressed his claim and Victor-Emmanuel bowed to the pressure. The Niçois were absolved of all loyalty towards Savoy and were asked to agree to change. On 22 April 1860, out of a possible 32,175 voters,

27,348 Niçois voted on annexation. An overwhelming majority – 27,003 – opted to join France

The polical realignment of 1860 was accompanied by an extraordinarily swift language shift and reorientation of cultural identity. Since 1562, when Emmanuel Philibert had ruled against Latin, public life had been predominantly in Italian and private life largely in Niçois. However, by 1865 Nice had become a community where Italian had been effaced in the public domain and where Niçois had come under attack as the language of family and conviviality. Such an enormous linguistic leap was atypically fast and complete, particularly given the difficulty in invoking a common past to legitimate the shift.

The reasons are interesting. The most influential seems to be economic. An important and sizeable business community was swayed by commercial consideration to be pro-French and to adopt this language on the grounds that it would encourage trade. A second factor was that the Niçois intelligentsia, like others throughout Europe, was already sensible to the attractions of French tradition and steeped in its culture, political thought and philosophy. A percentage of this group moved without regret or difficulty from using French as a prestigious lingua franca to using it exclusively in everyday life. A third source of pressure for the Niçois to adopt French came from the cosmopolitan community which frequented the town in the winter and whose members used French as lingua franca. Fourthly, many of the administrative class under Piedmont-Savoy rule, the soldiers, jurists, civil servants and professionals who used Italian in their working lives and who had constituted much of the Italian party, moved after annexation to other parts of Piedmont. Their places – and roles – were taken by incomers from France. The ruling élite became not only French-speaking but French. Finally, after joining France in 1860, the Niçois experienced the vigorous nation building undertaken by the Third Republic, including linguistic unification.

The economic reasons why commercial circles in Nice would tend to belong to the *parti français* were considerable. In 1853 the suppression of Nice's status as a free port, caused by pressure from other interest groups in Piedmont-Savoy, notably the Genoese, brought general dissatisfaction. Nice's poor agricultural hinterland meant the town was far from self-sufficient. Its dependence on imported goods (for example, Nice bought much of its wheat from Russia) had been exacerbated by tax exemptions on goods coming by sea (Bovis-Aimar and Malausséna, 1998). The alternatives, transporting goods over the Alps, to and from Turin, or trading across the border were either difficult or expensive. It was physically much easier to sell to France. Indeed, the main agricultural products of the region, olive oil and citrus fruits, were exported mainly to France (Latouche, 1951).

The Role of the *Parti Français*

All exports to France, however, attracted heavy import duties. Merchants saw an advantage in joining the French state which would open trading routes west across the Var and abolish duties and quotas. For these pragmatic reasons, the *gros négociants* and bankers constituted an important section of the *parti français*. They serviced both the commercial class and the foreign residents who came for the winter season. The business community was proved partly correct in its expectations that annexation by France would be advantageous and Nice expanded quickly in the 1860s. Property speculation in connection with the tourist trade brought new money and new enterprise. Access to the town was improved; for instance, the railway which had ended at Toulon was extended to Nice in 1864. The hinterland remained poor but large numbers of peasants came to work during the winter as maids and valets.

Economic growth and prosperity ensured the spread of French. The *gros négociants* had always been 'fortement influencés par la culture française' (Compan, 1989: 261) but, even if they had not been pro-French and willing to use the language, the indigenous Niçois had ceased to be relevant in a commercial class which, after 1860, assumed national, even international, dimensions. The Niçois represented, numerically and economically, a diminishing proportion of the commercial sector as possibilities for investment and enterprise attracted outside business interests to the town (Latouche, 1954). Increasingly Nice turned its back on the Italian peninsula with which physical communication remained difficult. Moreover, contact with Italy was discouraged as indicative of a seccessionist tendency.

Among intellectuals and the political élite other factors pertained, although the sociolinguistic effects were the same. Everything that had attracted the monarchs of Europe and those interested in new ideas, philosophies and technologies to French language and culture in the seventeenth and eighteenth centuries were also at play among the intelligentsia of Nice. This was true throughout Italy, where those committed to Italian unification acknowledged the French origins of some of their political thinking. It reveals much about the roles accorded to French and Italian that a spokesman of the *risorgimento*, Giuseppi

Ferrari, would write as a historian of the *risorgimento* in French (*Histoire des Révolutions d'Italie* [1858]) but as a polemicist and political activist in Italian.

The court of Piedmont-Savoy was in a singular position with regard to French influence. On the one hand Savoy, which was and always had been French-speaking, was the region in which the dynasty originated. On the other hand the intellectual and political élites of Piedmont-Savoy were on the whole conservative and hostile to the Republic and the Revolution. In the early part of the nineteenth century, if there was any feeling of commonality with France, it was with France of the *ancien régime*. As liberalisation was forced post-1848 on the monarch and the aristocracy, there was still great coolness towards French republican ideas.

Politically, the Niçois had three alternatives from which to choose during Italian unification: the revolutionary tradition of Mazzini or Garibaldi; the conservative tradition of the House of Savoy; or the republican tradition of France. The Niçois were not revolutionaries; despite the fact that Garibaldi had been born in the town, very few joined his forces. The conservatives supported Victor-Emmanuel because the House of Savoy had been cool towards political liberalisation. The radicals turned to France for the same reasons, namely that the Savoy monarchy had not been generally favourable to the new political currents of the nineteenth century and, despite changes apparent in the 1848 constitution, the liberal Niçois believed that political freedoms might be achieved more easily in the French state. It was ironic that, as events evolved, the conservative and catholic right should find itself supporting a monarchy which had at last accepted liberal reform and whose anti-clerical policies brought it into conflict with the papacy. It was equally ironic that pro-French liberal republicans should turn to an emperor who had taken power in a *coup d'état* and who supported the Pope.

The liberals expressed their opinions in French in the newspaper *L'Echo des Alpes Maritimes* which appeared in 1848 to lobby for the constitution. At first there was no suggestion of a break with Piedmont-Savoy (Ayache, 1978). This came three years later when the suppression of the free port was suggested and Turin repressed the town's discontent in an authoritarian manner. At this time the paper became unequivocally the organ of the *parti français*, taking the name *L'Avenir de Nice*, and campaigning energetically for the future to be French. It could be argued that many of the articles before the annexation demonstrate a desire to share in the prestige of being French, as well as the belief that there will be benefits. This motivation is thrown into relief after the defeat of 1870 when an element of doubt appears and there are reflections on what the French defeat will mean (*Avenir*, March/April 1860; *Messager de Nice*, 1870).

The Niçois of the conservative right were in the Italian party. A sizeable proportion of the aristocracy was linked closely to Piedmont by family ties, education and employment. For example, the Niçois who practised law, administered or taught knew their future was with Italy. They wrote pamphlets and made speeches and their newspaper, *Il Popolare Nizzardo*, made the case for remaining part of Piedmont-Savoy. However, this class came under enormous pressure to vote the 'right' way to allow Piedmont-Savoy to keep good relations with France. Interestingly, even in this group, there was widespread competence in French. As a group these people might not have wanted to be part of Napoleon III's empire, but individually they recognised the necessity of knowing French as a mark of their own education and sophistication.

The debate before the referendum was bitter. *Il Popolare Nizzardo* advanced the arguments for being part of the new Italy in which Piedmont-Savoy was playing the leading role. *L'Avenir* argued for 'reunion' with France. However, the debates through the press in Italian and French were for an educated minority. For the majority of people any debate took place in Niçois: 'Fait essentiel une fois de plus: les habitants de Nice et des bourgs littoraux expriment leur joie en nissart. Les campagnes de Press n'ont guère de prise sur eux' (Compan, 1989: 298).

Incomers and Language Change

Following annexation, the social composition of the town underwent profound change. For example, lawyers, doctors, teachers and administrators with diplomas from Italian universities were not recognised by the French and many left for Turin (Lubonis, 1871). The arrival of functionaries from France allowed the shift to French in public life to happen quickly. It was not simply that people changed their language habits; the speakers themselves changed.

However, incomers do not necessarily mean the death of a local language. The case of Catalan shows that incomers can be assimilated and the local language maintained even when it experiences the severest repression (Conversi, 1997). All the same, an essential difference between Catalonia and the County of Nice is the category of people who left and came. Nice lost its governing élite: one faction left and became part of the Italian tradition; the other faction stayed and became part of 'la

République Française, une et indivisible' in which regionalism was frowned on and in which Paris was a powerful magnet for those with ability and ambition.

Other strategies of nation building and linguistic unification – conscription and schooling – also played their part in the language shift in Nice. Conscription into the French army had first taken place between 1793 and 1814 and returned to Nice in 1860. The events of 1870–71 meant these conscripts were soon to fight for their new country. Experience in an army which did not organise battalions by region completed the linguistic shift which the education system had begun.

Education in Nice changed several times over the centuries. Italian was the official language of education for the period 1814–60, although French was the main foreign language. The Collegio became the Lycée Masséna in 1861 and secondary education was conducted in French. Compulsory primary education in the 1880s brought construction of more schools and ensured that all Niçois, not simply the élite, would pass through French education. It was perhaps the influence of the visitors in the winter which caused English and German to be taught as principal foreign languages in the lycées rather than Italian.

Further pressure on the Niçois to move both politically and culturally under the umbrella of the French came from the Catholic church which firmly supported annexation. This was partly because the Catholic church had always organised itself with little regard for political frontiers. But it was primarily because of the antagonism of the church to Italian reunification, by which the papacy would lose territory and influence, that the church favoured annexation. The chilly relationship with Piedmont-Savoy, contrasted with the church's good relations with Napoleon III, led to the clergy being among the most enthusiastic proponents of the Niçois accepting French citizenship and adopting French language and identity. The seminary which was restored to the town in 1815 had a reputation for the 'snobisme de certains ecclésiastiques à s'exprimer dans la langue des philosophes' (Compan, 1989: 260). L'abbé Briffod took the opportunity to eulogise French in a speech to prize winners at the seminary in 1862. He proffered arguments which would be rejected by present-day linguists but which were important to his audience of whom many did not have French as their first language:

> L'ordre logique de la phrase, cette marche directe si favorable à la clarté, cette horreur de l'inversion, cette simplicité dans l'arrangement des mots, qui semble ne se soumettre qu'à leur ordre métaphysique,

enfin cette lucidité qui, se prêtant ensuite aux définitions de la philosophie et à la grâce facile des relations sociales, a fixé pour toujours le génie propre à la langue française. (Briffod, 1862: 22)

Another cleric, the Abbé Tisserand, wrote a *Histoire de Nice et du département des Alpes-Maritimes* published shortly after annexation. In it, he calls Nice 'ce petit coin de la France' (Tisserand, 1862: vi).

The final factor that pushed the Niçois into accepting France and French came from the fact that they were perhaps the first people to experience tourism. In other words, they were used to contact with a cosmopolitan community. The aristocratic habit of spending the winter in Nice grew from modest beginnings in the early years of the eighteenth century. At first the visitors were mainly British; by the time of the annexation the international community in Nice numbered between 10–12,000 from all over Europe (Alziary de Roquefort, 1865). French was widely used as the principal lingua franca both in aristocratic circles and by their staff in their dealings with locals (Latouche, 1951). The Niçois who wished to profit from tourism were obliged to use French. The acceptance of French as the lingua franca is illustrated by various documents, including a letter in French – not the customary Italian – to Victor-Emmanuel from a pressure group which opposed construction of a casino (Hallez d'Arros, 1849). Advertisements and guide-books also appeared in French. Writers at the time regretted that the townspeople were so influenced by the visitors that they wished to adopt their language (Bonifacy, 1830). Such a reaction evokes comparison with contemporary French newspaper editorials and letters which rail against the present influence of Anglo-Saxon language and culture.

Conclusion

After 1860, Italian was replaced by French for all formal purposes. However, the language shift in Nice was eventually to be more than a simple exchange of one official language for another (the H languages in Ferguson's 1959 notation of diglossia).

Nissart at first retained a presence in the town buoyed by literary activity which lasted through the nineteenth century. Poems, plays and songs by Rancher, Guisol, Emanuel, Rondelli, Eynaudi, Genari and Gag played a central role in local Nissart culture. This renaissance of Nissart literature was, however, at odds with the linguistic unification taking place elsewhere. Nice was becoming inexorably a French town, both because of the linguistic dilution caused by the numbers and social influence of French-speaking incomers and because individuals and families decided to adopt French on account of the prevailing nationalism as well as social mobility, commercial advantage and prestige.

The process was swift among the middle class but slower among the working class where language loyalty was stronger, particularly in certain tightly knit groups in the town. In the market and the abattoir, for example, Nissart persisted until the Second World War. In the more inaccessible parts of the mountains, shepherds and farmers also held to their traditional language, gavouòt. Such speakers remained numerically a small minority and, in terms of political influence, unimportant. Eventually radio, television and easier communications, combined with the influence of education and conscription, caused these last pockets of local language to shift to French, in exactly the same way as many other minority language groups both in France and elsewhere. Cavour, Victor-Emmanuel's prime minister, in his effort to promote the Plombières deal, had underlined 'les affinités de race, de langue et d'intérêts' of the Niçois and the French. In fact these affinities were not with French but with the other dialects of Occitan which were under attack by the nation-building policies of the French state. Thus the Niçois chose to become French-speakers and, at the same time, to discard their specificity. That they did so testifies as much to the attraction of the French-speaking world as to the pressure brought to bear by French authorities. The latter without the former does not necessarily lead to language shift, as any history of Catalonia illustrates.

At the end of the twentieth century Nissart remains, but simply in a heritage role. Classes in Nissart have been held since 1954, when the lycée Masséna offered it for one hour a week following the Deixonne legislation permitting regional languages in schools. Politicians, particularly the Medécin family, have used it judiciously to certain audiences to mark their roots in the town. Road names in the old town are now given both in Nissart and French and the town hall publishes a bilingual magazine. An indication, however, of how little Nissart means to the present Niçois was revealed by research conducted early in 1999 which showed that 90% of people using the Nice bus service did not recognise that their timetable was given both in French and Nissart. They believed it was in French and Italian for the benefit of tourists. Nothing suggests that Nice will witness a successful revival of Nissart on the pattern of other border communities such as the Catalans and the Basques.

References

Ayache, G. (1978) *Histoire des Niçois*. Paris: Nathan.

Bonifacy, Abbé (1830) *Notes et Copies de Documents sur Nice et le Comté*. Bibliothèque de Cessole, folios 73–102.

Bovis-Aimar, M. and Malausséna, P. (1998) Correspondances d'affaires de la banque Carlone 1858–1861. In *Nice Historique*, No. 3, 151–9.

Briffod, Abbé de (1862) *Empire et Conquêtes de la Langue Française, Discours Prononcé à la Distribution des Prix du Petit Séminaire de Nice*. Nice: Caisson.

Compan, A. (1989) *Histoire de Nice et de Son Comté*. Nice: Serre.

Conversi, D. (1997) *The Basques, the Catalans and Spain*. London: Hurst.

d'Hombres, G. (1877) Une notice historique sur le comté de Nice. In *Histoire de France*. Paris: Delagrave.

de Roquefort, A. (1865) Le high life à Nice. In *Les Hivers de Nice: Impressions et Souvenirs*. Nice: Gauthier.

Ferguson, C. (1959) Diglossia. *Word* 15.2, 325–40.

Hallez d'Arros (1849) *Requête au Roi de Sardaigne sur le Projet de Fonder à Nice une Maison de Jeux*. Nice: Caisson.

Latouche, R. (1951) *Histoire de Nice I*. Nice: Ville de Nice.

Latouche, R. (1954) *Histoire de Nice II*. Nice: Ville de Nice.

Lubonis, L. (1871) *Notes, Lettera 3, Lubonis Family Papers*. Bibliothèque de Cessole, Nice.

Tisserand, Abbé de (1862) *Histoire Civile et Religieuse de la Cité de Nice et du Département des Alpes-Maritimes*. Nice: Visconti et Delbecchi.

Chapter 8

The French Language, Universalism and Post-colonial Identity

MIKE HOLT

Most debate on European linguistic identity confines itself to the *Staatsnationen* of Europe. However, the boundaries of European influence do not end at Gibraltar and the Bosphorous, as the colonial legacy has left its impact much further afield. In particular the colonial powers of Britain and France tried not only 'mythically expanding the nation into a transhistorical, and thus eternal, entity' (Wodak *et al.*, 1999: 1) through a reconstruction of their own histories, but also through a real expansion in territory and linguistic influence. In fact, it has been argued that a main part of the thrust of modernism was to make the European model a blueprint for all societies (Sayyid, 1997). Algeria is indeed a case in point. Up until independence in 1962 it was considered by the French as a part of France and therefore of Europe. This has left an important cultural legacy which has complicated the issue of linguistic identity. This has led to a marked and often bloody conflict over the relationship between French, Arabic and other indigenous languages which is far from resolved. It is the aim of this chapter to examine the roots of this conflict and the shifts in the balance of power between the main protagonists.

What is striking about linguistic conflict in Algeria is that these two main protagonists, French and standard Arabic, both base their claims to be the vehicle for Algerian identity on their universalist credentials. For those who support French, it is the language *par excellence* of rationality, clarity and modernity and joins Algeria to the wider French-speaking world, although Algeria is not formally a member of the Francophonie. On the other hand Arabic can claim a unique place as the language Allah chose to reveal the Quran as a message of eternal and universal truth to the last prophet Muhammad. A part of the proof that the Quran is divinely inspired is its inimitability which translations into other languages cannot hope to match. Neither language is, of course, strictly speaking indigenous to Algeria and hence the necessary recourse to universalist arguments. Moreover, Algeria does not fall neatly into two linguistic camps. In addition to those in favour of an imported model are those seeking a regional or specifically Algerian identity through the Berber language, Amazighe, or through the Algerian dialectal form of Arabic which is markedly different from standard Arabic.

Before discussing French universalism and later attempts to promote indigenous languages it would be both more helpful and chronologically accurate to begin with the universalist traditions of Arabic because these were well established before the arrival of the French. Most large towns had Muslim scholars or *'ulama'a* who helped to preserve religious orthodoxy and, at the same time, maintain the study of classical Arabic as a prerequisite for textual exegesis, particularly of the Quran and Hadith. Outside these groups of scholars, nearly all of whom were based in urban areas, the countryside remained largely ignorant of classical Arabic but spoke either a highly divergent colloquial Arabic or one of the Berber languages. So, classical Arabic functioned as a mainly liturgical language rather like Hebrew before the creation of the state of Israel; no-one spoke it as a mother tongue but small groups of specialists were highly trained in its use and interpretation and thus occupied a privileged position in urban society.

Many of the *'ulama'a* had been trained abroad in famous centres of Muslim learning such as Al-Azhar in Cairo and Zaitouna in Tunis. Irrespective of their origins they studied the same sacred texts, the same rules of grammar and shared the same views on Muslim worship and the observation of its rituals. This helps explain why, despite widespread rural variation, urban Islam has remained remarkably homogeneous throughout the Muslim world: the *'ulama'a* acted as guardians of both the religion and linguistic standardisation. So classical Arabic had universalist claims not because it was widely used and understood throughout the Arab world but because it was the language of the sacred texts, of the schools of law and jurisprudence and of the religious specialists who interpreted this canon for the population at large. As Benedict Anderson says, 'large religious communities are only imaginable through the medium of a sacred language and script ... and the further it was from speech the better: in principle everyone has access to a pure world of signs' (Anderson, 1983: 12).

Furthermore, Muslim rulers derived their legitimacy from Islam rather than from ethnicity or lineage and yet were unable to challenge the *'ulama'a* over matters of religion. The *'ulama'a* in turn had little influence over executive decisions. The result was that both religion and language remained untainted by dynastic corruption and worldly interests. Classical Arabic was then a divinely chosen vehicle which expressed universal spiritual values but which was not compromised by any link with temporal power. In fact, the relative autonomy of both Arabic and Islam is part of its current appeal when popular confidence in the secular regimes of North Africa and the Middle East is at an all-time low (Holt, 1996).

French Universalism

The French version of universalism had very different origins. Although it often carries strong republican overtones, it predates the revolution but is still very much connected to political power. Many cite the Ordonnances de Villers-Cotterets of 1539 as the beginnings of both standardisation and universalisation of French. These edicts were issued during the reign of François I and made French the language of both justice and administration in place of Latin. Indeed, Lafont (1968) argues that the Jacobins merely completed the work of previous monarchs. But the impetus to replace Latin and to universalise French does not appear out of thin air. Nor can there be a purely French explanation for this because practically the whole of Europe went through a vernacularising revolution in which Latin was replaced by spoken vernaculars which eventually acquired the fixity and elaboration of function of Latin. Anderson's (1983) account best explains in global terms the process by which this took place. Briefly, he sees the emergence of vernaculars as national languages as a result of the convergence of several historical developments, principally the invention of print combined with capitalism and with the inescapable fact of linguistic diversity.

Linguistic unification of Europe was always unlikely when so many languages were spoken and where there are major fault lines between Germanic, Slav and Romance families. But the invention of print caused capitalists to look for new markets once the printing and sale of Latin classics had reached saturation point. They turned instead to the vernaculars but, because of economies of scale, could not base new popular literacy on small regional varieties but rather on vernacular forms with larger market appeal. These developments helped create print communities which were the precursors of Anderson's 'imagined communities', the term he uses for modern nations. People saw themselves as belonging to a wider unseen community because they shared a print-language and later read the same daily national newspapers. Often, as is the case with France, administrative vernaculars came before the impact of print-capitalism but national impulses and consciousness only really developed with print.

For France and French to develop a national vernacular and then envisage its spread beyond the hexagon required something in addition to this national development. In part this was a result of its success as a diplomatic and cultural language, of the central position of France in Europe and of the subsequent adoption of French by the élite of Europe. Rickard reminds us that Rivarol's prizewinning essay, 'De l'universalité de la langue française', was not an argument proposing French as a universal language but an explanation of why and how it had come to be so (Rickard, 1989). It was only fitting that, having replaced Latin, French should claim some of its attributes of well-formedness, correctness, aesthetic beauty and, of course, universality. The Académie Française and then the Revolution helped to universalise French in the hexagon which inevitably involved the suppression of other languages such as Basque, Breton, Corsican and Occitan. But when this universalisation was applied across the Mediterranean to Algeria it was not in the same spirit of confidence and superiority.

After the defeat of 1870 at the hands of Prussia many began to doubt France's cultural and diplomatic supremacy. Much of the debate at this time agonises over the loss of influence and prestige and the remedy was to be a rapid colonial expansion combined with the *rayonnement* of French language and culture overseas (Sullivan, 1996). As Théodore Vibert said in 1887, 'si nous voulons conserver à notre race et à notre langue, leur rang légitime dans le monde, colonisons' (Ageron, 1978: 89).

But what was proposed in the Metropole was very different from what was delivered in Algeria. Firstly, before the official policy of *rayonnement*, came the systematic dismantling of local and traditional education through military campaign, confiscation of the funds used to support the Quranic schools, the closing down of others and the persecution of Quranic teachers. Faced with such an onslaught, the traditional Muslim education system, the sole provider of education in classical Arabic, all but collapsed. However, this was not then followed by universal schooling in French. Whatever was being said in Paris, when the *colons* came to realise that they would have to pay for the education of the *indigènes*, they refused. There are plenty of examples of naked colonial ambition such as the statement by Alfred Rambaud, Minister for Public Education, who said in 1898:

> La première conquête de l'Algérie a été accomplie par les armes et s'est terminée en 1871 par le désarmement de la kabylie. La seconde

conquête a consisté à faire accepter par les indigènes notre
administration et notre justice. La troisième conquête se fera par
l'école: elle devra assumer la prédominance de notre langue sur les
divers idiomes locaux, inculquer aux Musulmans l'idée que nous
avons nous-mêmes de la France et de son rôle dans le monde,
substituer à l'ignorance et aux préjugés fanatiques des notions
élémentaires mais précises de science européene. (Colonna, 1975: 40)

This not only reiterates the preoccupation with French in the world but
also refers obliquely to Arabic and Berber as 'divers idiomes locaux'
associated with ignorance and fanaticism and to be contrasted with the
precision and science of French. Despite this call to replace local
languages with French, by the 1920s less than 6% of school-age children
were being educated; what education they did receive was based on the
formula 'rien d'abstrait, rien de compliqué, rien de savant' (Morsly, 1984:
37). Many Muslim parents were also reluctant to send their children to
school because they saw it as incompatible with Islam, given the overtly
laic nature of French schooling. By 1954, on the eve of the war, after over
120 years of colonisation and after an official policy of *rayonnement* of
French language and culture, 90% of the Algerian population was
illiterate.

There had been a reform movement in Algeria dedicated to restoring
Islam and Arabic in a more nationalist framework, encapsulated in the
slogan 'Islam is our religion, Algeria is our country, Arabic is our
language' (Ageron, 1991: 94). However, this had little effect on literacy
levels and education as a whole. The low levels of education in French
conversely gave Francophone Algerians disproportionate power and
influence. Although the Front de Liberation National (FLN) used the
symbols of Islam, Arabic and *jihad* or Holy War to good effect, internal
communication was often in French. The reforming *'ulama'a* had
persuaded the FLN to agree to the restoration of Arabic in the
independent education system in 1961 but Algeria was faced with an
acute shortage of qualified teachers of Arabic after liberation. Arabs
from the East, mainly Egyptians, were recruited but did not prove
successful. Despite a supposedly universal Arabic, they did not
understand their pupils' dialect and the pupils had similar problems
with the Egyptian dialect. The largely French-educated FLN, although
nominally committed to arabisation, found it difficult to relinquish the
advantages French gave the party of government. Aziz Krichen's
description of the Tunisian bilingual élite could apply equally well to
Algeria:

... this modern intelligentsia was able to fight victoriously against foreign domination at the political level, but it turned out to be the best guarantor of the continuing hegemony at the linguistic and cultural level. The bilingual élite presented, and it represented itself, as a successful graft, a harmonious synthesis of opposing civilizing elements; in reality, in the intimacy of its being, it was spiritually submissive to Western values: it interiorized the inferiority of itself and the superiority of the other. (Krichen 1987: 301)

This was confirmed in an audit of the arabisation of Algerian administration carried out in 1975. Despite a law passed in 1968 stipulating that civil servants had to demonstrate an ability in Arabic, the audit found the majority of ministries working, training and disseminating information in French (Grandguillaume, 1983). Furthermore, although the entire primary system had been arabised by 1974, the universities were slow to follow suit and graduates from Arabic streams felt discrimination. So, despite an impressive programme of arabisation, the road to power and influence was still signposted in French. This led to strikes and demonstrations by *arabisants* in 1982. The régime's policy, post-independence, was to arabise from the bottom up, to pay lip service to arabisation at higher levels and to allow increasing influence from the *'ulama'a* in defining the content of the arabised curriculum in an attempt to outflank the left. In fact many Algerian secularists today attribute the rise of Islamism in Algeria to the ideological content of Arabic teaching, influenced as it was by these conservative religious elements.

This explanation is not wholly satisfactory, however, as many other Muslim countries, with very different histories, Arab and non-Arab, have also witnessed the rise of Islamism. It could therefore be explained in more global terms as part of a process of de-centring the West (Sayyid, 1997). This is a greater challenge for European notions of universality, both linguistic and political, because many both inside and outside the West no longer accept the validity of a basically European model of culture, progress and organisation. The reference to those inside the West is particularly appropriate here. Robert Young (1990) traces the emergence of postmodern thought to the fallout from the Algerian war of independence itself and to the influence it had on leading French intellectuals such as Satre, Derrida, Althusser and Lyotard.

Non-western Models

It now seems that the majority in Algeria, and especially the younger generation, has now rejected any form of French universalism, including of course the French language. As Olivier Roy says, 'l'universalisme religieux a tué l'universalisme tout court' (1992: 17). Many have opted for another non-western model which has much deeper resonance for them, hence the overwhelming victory in the first round of the general elections in 1992 for the Islamist FIS party. The secular, often French-educated FLN, having used both religion and language to bolster its position, was unable to stop the trend. In December 1990 there was the bizarre spectacle of FLN delegates voting in favour of total arabisation including parliamentary debate when most were more comfortable in French than Arabic. In fact, the law on arabisation bears a striking similarity to the Toubon law on the use of French in France. The official French translation of the Algerian law states: 'La langue arabe est une composante de la personnalité nationale authentique et une constante de la nation'.[1] Compare this with the Loi Toubon: '... la langue française est un élément fondamentale de la personnalité et du patrimoine de la France'.[2] And yet, despite the prevailing trend away from the West, the French language in Algeria remains remarkably resilient.

From independence until 1988 the press was controlled by the regime which not only monitored the content of publications but also ensured that circulation was higher for the Arabic-language press than for the French. After widespread rioting in 1988, the press was opened up and a multitude of titles in both languages, and also in Berber, emerged. It now appears that sales of French-language papers outsell the Arabic press (Arsenault-Leers, 1991). Many complain that the Arabic press is rendered in 'la langue de bois', empty rhetoric, whilst claiming the French papers have a higher intellectual content and are better presented and edited. Many Algerians still watch French television on satellite, dubbed 'les paradiboliques' by Islamists. Furthermore, despite the arabisation of most university courses, a large proportion of academic articles are still in French.

Perhaps understandably, the size of Algeria's Francophone population is exaggerated in France. To say that one-third of Algerians speak French may be literally true but at a basic level it is deliberately misleading; practically all Algerians speak either Algerian Arabic or Berber. Given that school pupils now choose between English and French, and for only two hours per week, it is less likely that future intellectuals and readers will be attracted to the French press in the same way. But the use of French for information, entertainment, and as a language of wider contact, particularly with African states and with the Algerian diaspora, will not disappear simply because a majority of political parties find it politically expedient to denigrate it. Many well-known Algerian writers, such as Taher Djaout, have written in French and eloquently defended their right to do so, pointing out that it is possible to develop an Algerian identity in another language. Djaout likens French to booty captured during the war.

There are of course other languages claiming a right to represent national identity; up to a quarter of Algerians are Berber and yet the language has only just begun to gain recognition. Berbers have been the most vociferous opponents of what they see as arabisation on the cheap: 'l'arabisation au rabais'. This has led to a series of protests known as the Berber Spring and also a massive rally of some 500,000 against the arabisation law. At a meeting between all major opposition parties in 1996, not attended by the military government, an *entente nationale* was produced. The first article concerning national identity recognised *Amazighité* as one of the three principal components of this identity; the other two being Arabism and Islam.

In the past the FLN and the FIS have objected to a Berber identity, either because it threatens national cohesion or because it is irrelevant when the master signifier is Islam. Yet it is the only truly indigenous language in Algeria and has incontestable claims to authenticity. More recently writers such as the linguist Mohammed Benrabah have been arguing for Algerian Arabic as a national language which, he claims, fulfils both requirements of authenticity and modernity (Benrabah, 1992). As any chosen variety would be much closer to the language the majority speaks (many Berbers are bilingual), this would at first appear sensible. But the political fallout would be immense and there is no clear popular support for such a proposal. Algeria would be isolated from the other 20 states in the Arab League, and many Muslims in Algeria and abroad would see such a move as an act of apostasy to sever links with the language of the Quran. And, as is often the case with languages without an accepted orthography or literature, many Algerians see it as an inferior, corrupted and bastardised form of Arabic.

It would appear then that the French form of universalism is running into trouble. French never was sufficiently universalised in Algeria to form a popular base and the post-independence political and intellectual climate was against it. It is still widely used but has little overt political support and is likely to become less influential as it is no longer supported by the Algerian education system.

Standard Arabic, more surprisingly, still has its detractors and not only among the Berbers. Although it is the obvious candidate for a national language, it does not offer any specifically Algerian identity, a problem that all Arab states share with regard to nation building. Some of the associated problems which beset Standard Arabic in Algeria are of historical origin and related to poor pedagogy, the low literacy levels after years of French suppression, and the perceived ideological content of teaching material. It is now, however, better taught and to more students than ever before and some, particularly Islamists, insist on trying to use it in daily conversation.

For the reasons briefly mentioned above, a purely national solution in the form of Algerian Arabic is unlikely to succeed; however, Amazighe has a strong regional presence and official cross-party support which should secure its future as one of the main components of Algerian identity. Nearly 40 years after independence, French still plays a role in national life and yet can make no claims to represent national identity. Nor can it rely on universalist arguments now the West is no longer accepted as the uncontested model of human progress. Standard Arabic will undoubtedly carry the banner of Algerian identity for the foreseeable future although paradoxically it also has no specifically Algerian pedigree.

Notes
1. Plate-Forme de l'Entente Nationale from: ALGNEWS@GWUVM.BITNET
2. Loi no 94-665 du 4 août 1994 relative à l'emploi de la langue française, *Journal Officiel de la République Française*, 5 août 1994.

References
Ageron, C.-R. (1978) *France Coloniale ou Parti Colonial?* Paris: Presses Universitaires de Paris.
Ageron, C.-R. (1991) *Modern Algeria: A History from 1830 to the Present*. London: Hurst.
Anderson, B. (1983) *Imagined Communities: Reflections on the Origins and Spread of Nationalism*. London: Verso.
Arsenault-Leers, C. (1991) Fin de quelques taboos culturels en Algérie. *Le Monde Diplomatique* (June).
Benrabah, M. (1992) La modernité passe par l'arabe algérienne. *Hebdo libéré numéro 63*, 10–16 June.
Colonna, F. (1975) *Instituteurs Algériens: 1883–1939*. Paris: Presse de la Fondation Nationale des Sciences Politiques.
Grandguillaume, E. (1983) *Arabisation et Politique Linguistique au Maghreb*. Paris: Maisonneuve.
Holt, M. (1996) Divided loyalties: Language and ethnic identity in the Arab world. In Y. Suleiman (ed.) *Language and Identity in the Middle East and North Africa*. Richmond: Curzon Press.

Krichen, A. (1987) *La Tunisie au Présent, une Modernité au-dessus de tout soupçon.* Paris: CNRS.

Lafont, R. (1968) *Sur la France.* Paris: Gallimard.

Morsly, D. (1984) L'Enseignement du français et de l'arabe en Algérie pendant la période coloniale. In C. Achour *et al.* (eds) *Réflexions sur la Culture.* Algiers: Office des Publications Universitaires.

Rickard, P. (1989) *A History of the French Language.* London: Unwin Hyman.

Roy, O. (1992) *L'Échec de l'Islam Politique.* Paris: Éditions du Seuil.

Sayyid, B.S. (1997) *A Fundamental Fear: Eurocentrism and the Emergence of Islamism.* London: Zed Books.

Sullivan, K. (1996) Discourses of Language and Nation in Britain and France 1870–1914. Unpublished PhD thesis. University of Manchester.

Wodak, R., de Cillia, R., Reisigl, M. and Liebhart, K. (1999) *The Discursive Construction of National Identity.* Edinburgh: Edinburgh University Press.

Young, R. (1990) *White Mythologies: Writing History and the West.* London: Routledge.

Chapter 9

'It's a Culture Thing': Children, Language and 'Boundary' in the Bicultural Family

MICHAEL ANDERSON

Historically, anthropological research and scholarship began by examining particular forms of kinship ties and family relationships in particular locations around the world – families within cultures. What is considered here is the contemporary reversal of this – cultures in families.

It has become commonplace to talk of the collapse of political barriers in the European Community. It has also become commonplace to talk of the resultant economic and political consequences. Hence questions as to the meaning of Europe in terms of peoples' identities impose themselves with ever greater urgency and increasing complexity. Identity, explicit and implicit, invariably impinges forcefully on individual consciousness at times of social and cultural change. One particular dynamic underlying this perception is captured by social anthropologist Sharon McDonald:

> On the one hand it might seem that as borders become weaker – as people and goods traverse them more easily – there will be a consequent relaxing of the sense of allegiance to place and people, [but] very often the reverse is actually the case. Notions of 'us' and 'them' become stronger still (1993: 1).

In other words, 'others' may become more 'other' the closer they are. Distant sociocultural difference remains exotically and conveniently blunt while encroachment or symbiosis renders it far sharper and liable to cutting. However, this chapter is not about ethnic tensions and racism. It is about voluntary inter-national, inter-cultural marriages and family relationships. Its point is to illustrate ethnographically, in the most intimate of social contexts (the family home), the point made by

McDonald that, despite an anticipation that allegiances to place and people might diminish as national and cultural borders weaken, one may, as a result, become 'othered' in one's own home.

Borders, Boundaries and Symbols

Anthropologists and other social scientists tend to attribute the concept of boundary to the work of Frederick Barth (1969) and to his theorising of the organisation of cultural difference. Cultural identity, he argued, was not best examined in cultures, as of their contents, but at their edges, or 'boundaries'. However, as Cohen has since argued, when anthropologists define their focus of enquiry they implicitly, if inadvertently, locate boundary at the centre of their concern. Indeed, the concept is intrinsic to the history (and success) of the discipline: 'The relativism of anthropologist/anthropologised, us/them, self/other clearly *implies* boundary' (1994: 122) [my italics].

Anthropology's preoccupation with the concept as the location of marked difference between the contents of cultures, as the place of cultural endings and beginnings, has, argues Cohen, been at the expense of differences between individuals. In other words, anthropology's homogenising of collectivities and traditional disregard for the individuals which comprise them has led to the mere determination of the latter as an invariant product of the former.

This is not to say that diversities in cultures have not been recognised. However, describing how these diversities fit together has neither been appreciated nor acknowledged as critical to social and cultural theory. Far from being an integration of diversities, Cohen describes culture as an aggregation, thus permitting within culture broad differences of sociality and individuality. Notwithstanding the importance of this point, I admit to being in some sense guilty of perpetuating the former model. But this is only insofar as it remains an accurate portrayal of the individuals who populate the text and the field of which it is a description – ordinary people who themselves use homogenising models of culture in the contexts of their interpersonal relations to articulate their own and other individual identities. It is in this context that I adopt as a title the phrase 'It's a culture thing'.

'It's a culture thing' is borrowed from a British woman living in Greece and raising what she described as her 'half British, half Greek' child – the child's father being Greek. The phrase captures what the woman referred to as the issues of raising a child in a cultural context with which she was less familiar than the rest of her family, and where differing views on bringing up a child were often explained in terms of culture and culture difference.

What I perhaps somewhat inadequately and even inaccurately describe as 'bicultural families', families where children have parents of different nationalities, languages and cultures within Europe, gives rise to practical questions of childraising and theoretical questions of child, mother, father and grandparental identities.

'Identities' or identity is used here in the contemporary social anthropological sense as to how the individual is conceptualised in a particular cultural concept both by the subject and by those around, rather than merely as a feature or a position in social structure (i.e. class, occupation, age, gender, etc.). This might be, for instance, how the child, mother, father or grandparent in a bicultural family engage (or are engaged) in processes and complexities of selfhood and belonging; how this is expressed and how agitated. This chapter offers evidence for and reflection on the curious notion of 'boundaries' between cultures yet within the intimate domestic context of the family.

Broadly speaking, so-called cultural differences are manifested symbolically. That is to say (taking symbolic to be virtually anything in some sense meaningful or interpretable) that sounds, artefacts and actions are (or can be) interpreted quite differently between different groups of people but in a similar manner among their respective members. Rather than being factual, symbols are multivocal (Turner, 1967); they are individually interpreted (Geertz, 1971) and, to those who use them, they are by their very nature malleable and manipulable (Cohen, 1994: 17). In other words, symbols are ambiguous and enigmatic for analytical enquiry, if unambiguous and clear for making sense of particular lives.

Cohen has argued that, unlike frontier and border, boundary is not a static geographical, political or ethnic fact. Rather it is about conscious-ness – consciousness about self as a social being in a particular social, political, ethnic or geographical context. Boundary may well interplay with frontier and border in a given situation but analytically, Cohen argues (1994: 131), the distinction is crucial. Because boundary is far more about consciousness (subjectivity and meaning) than about fact, it retains the elusiveness and enigma of symbolism. As such, the specific subjective meanings which a boundary – like a symbol – evokes in individuals for whom those meanings are easily communicable are far from coherent or transparent.

Boundaries are more or less conceptual 'zones' for reflection on 'who one is' and 'who others are' (1994: 128). They are not necessarily places or lines but a perception of difference experienced and/or expressed through a tangible form; imagery, language, law, lore and so on. Moreover, as components of the zone, these tangible aspects of difference are themselves subject to dynamic processes of change and alteration. They emerge, evolve and are superseded, being continually subject to differing uses and interpretations even among those who, at any rate superficially, are individually aggregated by them and collectively differentiated from others through them.

Apart from looking at particular familial circumstances, in which boundary processes are rendered active, the chapter also introduces the notion of the child as boundary. The child is a zone for – and of – reflection and a tangible symbol for parental (and grandparental) cultural claims from the perspective of those adults who are responsible for its care. Furthermore, rather than being a mere recipient of cultural transmission, common in social scientific writing on children, the child is also reconstituted as a field for competing adult identities. What will be shown in the case of the bicultural family is how boundary, as the zone of cultural contestation, is embodied in the person of the child and how, despite perceptions that cultural movement and human fluidity result in the disappearance or diminishing of boundaries at one level of analysis, they paradoxically reappear in another – the family.

Migrancy and movement round the world have increased markedly over the last two centuries. It has been suggested that between 1800 and 1914 net migration from Europe was around 50 million (Standing, 1984: 15). In 1984 more than half a million people moved legally to the United States from Mexico, the Philippines and Vietnam. Europe also has seen an increase in social movement and in the number of immigrants, especially in Germany, France, the United Kingdom and Scandinavia. In Sweden more than one in eight people was born in a foreign country. In Germany there is estimated to be over three-quarters of a million Greeks, over half a million Italians and well over 100,000 Portuguese. Over 15,000 Britons live in Greece.

Transnational movement is a common global feature of the late 20th century. From intrepid nomadic individuals to forcefully displaced masses, migration is described by a range of commercial and political categories; economic migrant, tourist, ex-patriot, refugee, professional nomad, globalisation, mixed race, hybrid, and so on. All are testimony to the vocabulary that has emerged from transnational movement and to the fact that it is no longer extraordinary. Such movement has added impetus to an increasing sense of cultural fluidity. There is movement away from the world of fixed cultures and bounded particularities towards one which relies on the more permeable transparent differences between them.

This description is generally valid for the entire world (depending which social aspect is being addressed) but is particularly true of the European continent where, for example, official border controls have largely ceased to function as they did some years ago. Individuals and artefacts, ideas and images exchange and cross-fertilise at will. Travel, tourism, television, telephones and on-line encounters with erstwhile 'others' are now an accepted part of everyday life. The global village is further condensed into the global household as access to lives and places lie literally at the touch of a button.

The volume of scholarly social scientific literature attempting to depict transnational movement has increased proportionately (Chambers, 1994; Hannerz, 1996; Rapport, 1997: 64–79; Dawson and Rapport, 1998). Other disciplines have also sought to capture the experience of individuals and groups (Bammer, 1994; Robertson *et al.*, 1994) both in transit and displaced. The words, thoughts and feelings of these people signify and embody processes quintessentially of our times. These writers, along with others, provide us with images of a world in which borders are no longer simply symbols of exclusion but invitations to go beyond a particular spatio-social locality, invitations to impact elsewhere by means of oneself and to be impacted by others. Affordability and profitability, along with the frequency and intensity of virtual encounters, have largely nullified the fear of exotic cultural difference and have rendered it welcoming. Social anthropologist Clifford Geertz captures this with his description of the movement of myths, languages, music, imagery, decor, costume, furnishings and, above all, persons (Geertz, 1986: 120–1). These have changed even the most isolated geographical areas and made them places of global, social interaction.

If national borders are becoming increasingly permeable then arguably this has been precipitated and followed by cultural boundaries becoming increasingly transparent. Indeed, anthropologists have begun to check themselves when talking of the world in terms of plural cultures. Hannerz (1993: 68), for example, asserts there is a 'new diversity of interrelations, fluid and without edges'. This, he insists, must be the alternative to 'a global mosaic of cultures; bounded, separate and distinct'.

Families and Cultures

Social movement correlates with the increasing incidence of what may be (inadequately and paradoxically) termed transcultural marriages. That is, marriages between individuals from different parts of the world. Bolstered by the decreasing threat of otherness and elsewhere in distant locations, individuals seek or stumble on special others with whom they form exclusive romantic, moral and legal relationships.

The presence of individuals from different cultural backgrounds generating the same family unit reverses the historical and relatively simple social scientific model of families in cultures. Moreover, unlike the legal and political vocabulary mentioned above in describing social movement, the vocabulary of fluidity, transparency and flows, with which culture itself is increasingly depicted, begins to be seen as superficial in the context of such families.

While the lines between geographic locations appear permeable to the artefacts, ideas and people passing through them, the view is a relatively distant one proffered by the non-native armchair theorist. It is not a view proffered by the native, the subject, for whom the difference is 'there' in the next room, the adjacent seat or the words and actions of those to whom one is closest.

The research material and comments I draw on were gathered from ethnographic fieldwork conducted among Greek/British family households in Greece. The fieldwork mainly involved interviewing parents, grandparents and children and entailed observational and participatory techniques. Although the particular geographic location suggests a limited context, the comments and scenarios recorded from it can be more widely interpreted.

The following comments capture and condense issues and feelings to which family members gave expression. Many of the points are rationalised as issues of culture and culture difference rather than merely personal or interpersonal concerns. In other words, culture provides both an explanation and justification of specific and immediately pertinent issues and deflects them from the interpersonal conflict, despite particular persons populating the comments and narratives. The particularities of personhood are excused and dismissed as of little consequence since they are merely their cultures writ small.

The bicultural family provides a context in which the parent and child dynamic is not only the medium for cultural reproduction but also the barrier – identified by family members – to cohesive and smooth domestic relationships. Individual comments focus especially on language and its use in homes where two languages are available: Greek and English. Adult contests around these are played out and fought on the battlefield of the child who is not simply a repository for language and culture but is, in the sense discussed, a zone of cultural contention and thus an agent in the construction of parental identities.

Brenda (name changed) met Dimitri (name changed) approximately 13 years ago when Dimitri was a student at the University of Manchester in the United Kingdom. Their relationship developed and, after several years of living apart and vacational visits to their respective homes, they decided to marry and settle in Athens. Dimitri is a personnel manager for a shipping company owned by his father's brother. Brenda is not in paid employment and stays at home to look after their 11-year-old son, Yannie. The family lives in an apartment; below them is Dimitri's mother who, like most mothers-in-law in Greece (Danforth, 1991: 106–8), plays a significant part in family life. Her significance is evident not so much as a link in the running of family life as to the impact she has on each family member. Much of this relates to the raising of Yannie and to the focus on him as a child of split identity.

In the first of a series of comments which illustrate the contest for Yannie's cultural soul, Brenda recalls her reaction to her mother-in-law's insistent attention and efforts to keep away the sinister influences commonly alluded to among elderly (and not so elderly) Greeks:

> As soon as Yannie was born, Yiayia [her mother-in-law] was all over him, going like this – 'ftou ftou ftou' and everything. That's to keep away the evil eye. It didn't bother me at first but now it really annoys me. I think it frightens the children and [because it involves spitting] spreads germs. It's a superstition they have … if you say, like, a compliment then you have to go 'ftou, ftou, ftou' to stop the evil eye coming. It's just the culture, you know … a culture thing.

Brenda describes attitudes which are foreign to her, such as keeping the evil eye at bay (provoked, ironically, by a compliment; complimenting a child can be seen as a veiled vehicle for a curse, negated by spitting). Brenda attempts to explain the foreignness by putting it down to culture. The rationalisation is not just explanatory but almost magically renders the particular object of her *Angst*, her mother-in-law, not only beyond criticism but also justifiably so. Also, the child in question is a clear focus for the expression of adult cultural identity; the mother-in-law in attempting to deter the evil eye and Brenda in her distaste for this deterrent. Moreover, what is healthy for the child is seen in some sense as metaphysically good from the mother-in-law's perspective but as emotionally and physically unhealthy ('it spreads germs') from Brenda's.

The child's use of language is also conflictual and is contested for its assumed consequences for the child's future:

I want him to think that he does have a relationship to my culture, but I don't know how that will work out. At the moment he won't even speak English to me – we had an argument about it a few nights ago. Dimitri sometimes takes my side and sometimes hers [mother-in-law]. I feel sorry for him, but it's all to do with Yannie.

For Brenda, language is clearly intrinsic to, and inseparable from, her child's cultural identity and, by extension, her own. Brenda's reaction to Yannie's refusal to speak English is a clear indication of this and is interpreted as a threat by his mother. She contests the point keenly with her mother-in-law but with only oscillating support from her husband who is as likely to support his mother as his wife. The differences that seemed so transparent from her home in rural Derbyshire are suddenly not so distant but present, seriously divisive and of important personal and family consequence.

The threat of losing her child to a culture she feels is not hers is bolstered by the views of her mother-in-law who is equally pressured and challenged by Brenda's foreign presence which, despite being a motherly one, establishes a barrier between her and her grandson. Relationships between grandmothers and grandsons are of profound importance in Greek family relationships and are well documented and mythologised in the wider context of Greek society and culture. This gives impetus and poignancy to the view the mother-in-law offers about the situation. She comments:

She [Brenda] speaks to the boy [Yannie] in her language [English] so there will be more problems. She doesn't understand our ways and traditions in Greece so it caused a lot of problems. The young ones from other countries think they know everything about children but they don't know anything.

The mother-in-law laments a younger generation of mothers, particularly those from foreign countries, that are an increasingly visible feature of Greek society. She is clearly frustrated at what she perceives as arrogance: they 'think they know everything'. Arguably, for her, differences stem as much from generational suspicion as from xenophobia and the cultural baggage which foreigners bring with them. When she highlights language as a key factor it is xenophobia which appears most prominent. She continues: 'There are lots of arguments but she still speaks English to Yannie. She should speak Greek otherwise he won't know where he is'.

The reference to arguments makes explicit the conflict and tension over language. The mother-in-law expresses her feelings by emphasising the foreignness of Brenda and what she sees as a divisive situation brought about by her daughter-in-law and her insistence on relating to her grandson in a particular language. As Brenda intimated earlier, Dimitri performs as a kind of self-appointed arbitrator between wife and mother, a role with which he is not entirely comfortable but one which he chooses to express independently, particularly when it concerns his son:

> They [Brenda and his mother] argue a bit, but not as much as before. It was always about Yannie. I was in the middle ... if I decide for my mother then my wife would not speak to me for the rest of the day. Which language to use is a difficult question for us.

Dimitri alternates between the respective sides and territories defined by the cultural limits of each of the women in his life. Dimitri prefers to speak to Yannie in Greek and so in one sense votes with his feet. He mentions there are conflicts between the women how Yannie should be treated and, most importantly, which language should be used and why. Yannie is the human rope in a cultural tug-of-war, the embodiment of potential threat and difference. More accurately, perhaps, he is the cultural cover over the personal intransigence of which he is both catalyst and object.

Yannie is the main focus of the boundary within and the zone of reflection for other identities. Yet he himself appears calmly indifferent to the disputes, rather as the eye of the storm remains tranquil in contrast to the raging gale around it. Aware of the contentiousness of his presence or, more cogently, his words and actions, he reflects:

> I'm Greek but sometimes I feel English. I speak both languages. But it depends on the situation: if it is better for me to speak English then I do. If it's better to speak Greek then I speak Greek. Mostly I speak Greek which upsets my mum (if I speak English then Yiayia tells me not to). Usually it's what ever is best in the situation. I don't speak English much at the moment but I did a lot before. I think I am both English and Greek because I have a parent from each country. But sometimes I don't know what I feel like. I have friends in England and cousins so when I go there I can be English and when I am here I am Greek.

Yannie contextualises the variant identities he feels are available to him from different relational contexts and scenarios. He locates himself in time (now and when he was younger) and place (England and Greece) as these occur to him in relation to these contexts. These components of identity are pragmatically employed or conveniently discarded pieces of a personal and changing montage of belonging and are not, as in the case of his elders, matters of absolute significance.

In a Place and a Manner of Speaking

In a separate but comparable family a slightly different, but not uncommon scenario, unfolds. Margaret and Markos married 15 years ago after they met while Margaret was on holiday in Greece. Both are capable of speaking some of the other's language but their daughter Electra (12) shows how, in reality, the domestic politics of this are neither simple nor equally satisfactory:

> My dad used to speak English to my mum but now he only speaks Greek because he doesn't like English and my mum doesn't like speaking Greek. If he hears me speaking English he gets angry and tells me I'm Greek and I should speak Greek. So I only speak to mum in the bedroom where he can't hear us. So, in the bedroom we speak English and here in the sitting room we speak Greek. Sometimes when dad is upset he tells me to say things to mum and he tells me it in Greek so he doesn't have to speak English, then I tell it to mum in English.

Electra's description suggests not only a difference regarding which language should be spoken but also how the physical space of the home is sectioned off for a particular language. The use of different languages by children, where the mother tongue of the parents is different, is not unusual in bilingual families (Harding and Riley, 1986; Hornby, 1977) and frequently involves an arrangement whereby the child speaks to each parent in his or her mother tongue. In the situation described by Electra, however, this is a hostile arrangement. Nevertheless, Electra effects her own diplomatic compromise to deter uncomfortable reactions by not upsetting either parent in the language of the other by using it in the wrong place. In doing so, she shows awareness of her symbolic importance in the relationship which exists between her parents. However, their relationship is not something outside her and which she merely accepts as an isolated feature. Rather it is intrinsic to consciousness and a facet of self. As mediator she becomes, literally, the difference between her parents and therefore, for all intents and purposes, their cultures.

Dimitra, who is 13, comes from another family but one in which language is also a potent symbol of belonging and therefore of intense reflection and feeling. Dimitra describes an experience she had when younger:

When my mum came to meet me at school, I was so embarrassed because she couldn't speak Greek properly. My friends would say: 'She's not Greek. Why does she speak like that?' They started calling me 'Xeni' [foreigner]. So I told her not to come any more, or to wait in a different place.

The story is confirmed by Dimitra's mother who emphasises her own sense of alienation generated by the experience:

Dimitra said: 'Mum, why are you so stupid?' I couldn't believe it. I was so humiliated and hurt. In a way she was right. To her I was 'stupid'. That's how it must have seemed. It made me so ashamed. I thought I could speak Greek properly but they could still tell I was a foreigner. I started thinking what the hell am I doing here when my own child doesn't want me near her. After that she would only let me meet her where the others couldn't see me, but all the other mums were up by the gate.

Stupid, as Dimitra refers to her mother, not only describes how the child experiences her mother but also is an alienating, or 'othering', of someone who ought not to be othered. Ought not, for if anyone were familiar in the strictest sense of the word it should be one's mother. Dimitra's description, however, performs the functional – rather than symbolic – job she requires of it by underlining the exclusion of her mother from the critically embarrassing space she would otherwise occupy in the company of school friends and other school mums.

Dimitra is for her mother what Dimitra's mother is for her: a tangible cultural contradiction. Dimitra is her daughter but thoroughly and unashamedly Greek. Her compliance with the child's demand for expulsion is born not only of her own sense of inferiority but also of her feeling that her daughter will suffer because of her presence outside the school. The mother's view that she thought she spoke Greek 'well enough' is harshly checked and put back in its rightful and foreign place. All in all the mother is demoted and deported from the critical space of the school gate.

For Dimitra, identification with the school cohort and the pressure to conform to the tacit conditions of agreed norms (James, 1993: 140–3) cannot be overstated. James (1986, 1993) devotes considerable effort to stressing the dynamics of 'sameness', at least among British children. 'Those who are perceived to differ too much are ruthlessly identified and named' (James, 1986: 162). Dimitra's mother poses precisely this threat to the daughter's sameness to her school friends. The foreignness of the mother renders Dimitra potentially different if not already actually different. Dimitra's identification as 'Xeni' suggests this. Damage limitation is effected by the removal of her mother from those who 'other' Dimitra because of her mother.

Social Protocol

Family politics of polite social protocol and pressure to instil a cultural form of this into children encourages parents from contrasting cultural backgrounds to open domestic hostility even, or especially, over the most banal of daily exchanges. Pat, for example, speaks of when her daughter, Andrea, was seven:

> We went back to England for a holiday and I was trying to get Andrea to say please all the time, or when she was supposed to, because the kids here [Greece] tend not to say it that much. My father was appalled when she wouldn't say 'please' or 'thank you'. But when we came back to Greece, my husband Taki thought that she was being too formal. I tried to tell him that in England you have to say 'please' and 'thank you' a lot, otherwise it sounds rude. He said it was too formal and in Greece people are not so formal. He even thought it sounded sarcastic when Andrea kept saying 'please' and 'thank you' to him. It caused a lot of friction between us, and Andrea was just confused.

The comment suggests the sensitivity and potential for family *Angst* over what might otherwise appear relatively insignificant exchanges. Children's usage of 'please' and 'thank you' takes on a significance beyond their functions as mere expressions of request and gratitude; they become complex emblems of cultural contest and identity.

Taki adds to Pat's comments by describing the practical outcome:

> So now when Andrea talks to her mother, she will say 'please' and 'thank you', and when she talks to me she doesn't. So when she goes to England she won't sound rude. But here it is not necessary to say these things all the time. It's crazy.

'She won't sound rude' is the reason given for Andrea's parents to teach their daughter to say the right thing, in the right place and in the right circumstances. Her father's requirement that she should not appear over-formal or sarcastic is met by his refusal to inculcate what he sees as superfluous courtesies. Her mother's requirement is that she should not appear discourteous to her own family in Britain. The difference is addressed by a plan to encourage appropriate verbal protocol in appropriate situations. Pat envisages training her daughter to prepare for occasional visits to England. Thus Andrea should adopt a different attitude to linguistic rules of request and gratitude somewhere between the respective airports which separate the two countries and cultures.

In this scenario, Andrea is assumed to be a human receptacle for competing social artefacts, each to be pulled out at the appropriate time and place. Clearly she is also an agent for emerging and agitating adult sensitivities about their own identities, histories and complexes of belonging. In their efforts to secure a socially competent child (albeit in their own images) Andrea's parents attempt to counteract each other's view not only of who Andrea is but also of who they are.

Cooper describes the ordinary family home as 'made up of histories and possibilities. So, the empty house is full of spaces for the imagination, of hopes and opportunities. Changes are the acquisition of a history, a mirror to life. The home is a space replete with pasts and memories' (1990: 37). In the bicultural home, with respect to transmission of habits and values, the child's future is linked to parental pasts, but pasts which do not necessarily accord with the cultural store of social practice and thought. Moreover, these parental pasts are in fact presents, sensitised and made conscious by transnational movement and by their children.

The child in the bicultural family is a boundary, an embodiment, a symbolic condensation of family identity and transnational movement. The children in the scenarios recounted present a meeting point of cultural incongruities, a junction for adult complexes of belonging. As a zone of reflection and for contention about culture, the child is the field on which adult relationships and identities are played, made and broken, continually constructed, de- and re-constructed.

The bicultural home comprises not only culturally different pasts but, as the comments of the adults and children illustrate, highly conflictual ones – at least potentially. They are pasts and cultures brought into domestic conflict by transnational movement. Bammer's reflections on family transitions capture succinctly this sense of

> what we hold on to and what we let go [of]; what we translate ('carry over') at our peril and for our survival. It is a reflection on the ways in which these issues of peril and survival are different for those who, by force or by choice, are divided between different cultures. (1994: 92)

Even the diminishing of displacement for the parent over time (either through learning the local language or incorporation of native beliefs and values) does not necessarily blunt the sharp edges of cultural difference.

The paradox of sociocultural processes and their diminishing of perceived cross-cultural differences is a factor in the emergence of bicultural families. Movement, migrancy, the decreasing significance of national borders – especially in Europe – and the permeability of their respective cultural provinces provide the illusion that collective difference ceases to exist. However, what actually occurs is a shifting of difference. The perceived boundary, understood to lie between individuals delineated by nations and cultures, is transposed to lie between individuals delineated by families. But the boundaries in these families do not comprise disembodied, inanimate difference. They are, on the contrary, people and, as argued above, as likely as not to be children.

The relatively fluid transnational and transcultural processes which make bicultural families possible contrasts with the intercultural (personal) edginess of everyday domestic life. Such families provide an intriguing context for the consideration of the child and of language as boundary, as a zone for adult reflection on culture and identity.

References

Bammer, A. (ed.) (1994) *Displacements: Cultural Identities in Question*. Bloomington: Indiana University Press.
Barth, F. (ed.) (1969) *Ethnic Groups and Boundaries: The Social Organisation of Culture Difference*. London: George Allen and Unwin.
Chambers, I. (1994) *Migrancy, Culture, Identity*. London: Routledge.
Cohen, A.P. (1994) *Self-consciousness: An Alternative Anthropology of Identity*. London: Routledge.
Cooper, M. (1990) Making changes. In T. Putnam and C. Newton (eds) *Household Choices*. London: Future Publications.
Danforth, L. (1991) The resolution of conflict through song in Greek ritual therapy. In P. Loizos and E. Papataxiarchis (eds) *Contested Identities: Gender and Kinship in Modern Greece*. Princeton: Princeton University Press.
Dawson, A. and Rapport, N. (eds) (1998) *Migrants of Identity*. Oxford: Berg.
Geertz, C. (1971) *The Interpretation of Cultures*. London: Hutchinson.
Geertz, C. (1986) The uses of diversity. *Mich. Q. Rev* 25 (Summer), 105–22.
Hannerz, U. (1993) The cultural role of world cities. In A.P. Cohen and K. Fukui (eds) *Humanising the City*. Edinburgh: Edinburgh University Press.
Hannerz, U. (1996) *Transnational Connections*. London: Routledge.
Harding, E. and Riley, P. (1986) *The Bilingual Family: A Handbook for Parents*. New York: Cambridge University Press.
Hornby, P. (1977) *Bilingualism: Psychological, Social and Educational Implications*. New York: Academic Press.
James, A. (1986) Learning to belong: The boundaries of adolescence. In A.P. Cohen (ed.) *Symbolising Boundaries: Identities and Diversity in British Cultures*. Manchester: Manchester University Press.
James, A. (1993) *Childhood Identities: Self and Social Relationships in the Experience of the Child*. Edinburgh: Edinburgh University Press.

McDonald, S. (ed.) (1993) *Inside European Identities*. Oxford: Berg.
Rapport, N. (1997) *Transcendent Individual*. London: Routledge.
Robertson, G., Mash, M., Tickner, L., Bird, J., Curtis, B. and Putman, T. (eds) (1994) *Travellers' Tales: Narratives of Home and Displacement*. London: Routledge.
Standing, C. (1984) *Population, Mobility and Productive Relations*. World Bank Staff Working Paper 695. Washington: The World Bank.
Turner, V.W. (1967) *The Forest of Symbols: Aspects of Ndembu Ritual*. Ithaca: Cornell University Press.

Chapter 10

Language Use and Identity Among African-Caribbean Young People in Sheffield

LERLEEN WILLIS

In the Jamaican context, Creole exists as a continuum at one end of which is Standard Jamaican English (SJE) and, at the other, the more strongly africanised basilectal Creole with varying degrees of admixture inbetween (Bailey, 1971). Standard English is the language of administration and is identified with schooling and education, whereas Creole is stereotypically a reflection of the rural, uneducated poor who have probably only a basic education. In the British context, where Jamaican Creole (JC) exists side by side with standard and nonstandard forms of English, the ensuing linguistic variation can mean that racism and prejudice perpetuate the myth that Creoles are a reflection of the linguistic deficiency of their speakers.

This study deals with bilingualism among young people in the African-Caribbean speech community in Sheffield. It is based on empirical research into the speech of 15 African-Caribbean young people between the ages of 15 and 30+ and is founded on recordings made between 1992 and 1994. The young people in the study were found to speak local and standard varieties of English combined with Jamaican Creole of various kinds. The context of Creole was invariably one of code-switching (CS), in other words, both English and Creole were often juxtaposed in the same speech. It is intended here to look briefly at language use exhibited by the sample and to speculate both on the social significance of language behaviour and on factors which determine the degree to which they maintain Creole.

Though Jamaican Creole is generally regarded as a low-prestige language, and is stigmatised both in Britain and in its native Jamaica

(Whyte, 1977), it is a full language rather than a dialect (Hall, 1966). It is separate in identity from British English, though arguably occurring on a continuum with standard varieties of Caribbean English. Thus the terms of reference here are bilingualism rather than bidialectalism. This assessment of Creole status does not find universal accord among lay persons, especially Creole speakers themselves who have been taught to reject their language as 'broken English'. Nevertheless informants' perception of the ethnolinguistic vitality of their language and its role in demarcating their ethnic and/or group identity in an alien environment are crucial to the maintenance of this low-prestige code.

It follows from the above that Creole : English bilingualism in Britain plays a key role in defining the identity of its speakers, essentially that of being black African in a white society. Many young African-Caribbean people born in Britain experience the forces of law as hostile and believe institutions adopt a position which disadvantages them. Black people in Britain continue to be regarded as a problem (articulated by the right in its call for repatriation) or as victims, seldom as people in charge of their own destinies (Gilroy, 1987: 11). The African-Caribbean's attempt to carve a sense of identity in the British context is a challenge to resourcefulness and resilience. As Gilroy (1993: 1) suggests, 'striving to be both European and Black requires some specific forms of double consciousness' since both identities may be presented as mutually exclusive in racist, nationalist and ethnically absolutist discourses.

It is suggested here that factors such as the extent of integration into a local African-Caribbean social network, solidarity with a black identity and also a relatively critical and non-integrative orientation towards white society in general favour maintenance of Creole among young people in Britain. In addition to defining identity among younger speakers, this low-prestige language remains for its speakers a major vehicle of resistance to racism, exclusion from white society and an antidote to the lack of belonging in British society.

Immigration

Social dynamics of the African-Caribbean population in Britain as a whole and specifically in Sheffield can partly be explained through history. African-Caribbeans began coming to Britain in significant numbers from the early 1950s to 1961 (Peach, 1965, 1968, 1982; Holmes, 1982; Ramdin, 1987). Thereafter immigration controls led to a reduction in arrivals. Caribbean migrants came at the invitation of the British government chiefly to support post-war economic regeneration in view of the shortage of indigenous labour (Peach, 1965: 36). Settlement patterns were largely dictated by seasonal availability of work and internal migration in Britain (Peach, 1968). Here the indigenous population was tending to move from larger centres of population to smaller ones, thus creating accommodation gaps. African-Caribbeans therefore settled largely in urban areas of Britain and began moving to Sheffield from 1955 onwards as they became aware of labour shortages in the steel industry (Mackillop, 1980/81).

The African-Caribbean population of Great Britain as a whole currently stands at an estimated 499,964 which represents 0.9% of the total population (Owen, 1996: 88). In Sheffield, this figure is in the region of 6,800 people (Census, 1992). Measured against the population of Sheffield as a whole, recorded as 501,202 (Census, 1992), the African-Caribbean population represents 1.4% of the total population of the city.[1] Since this figure includes two ethnic categories, black Caribbean and the anomalous black 'other', included in the census for the first time in 1991, it is difficult to verify precise figures.[2] Of the 2,397 Sheffield-based African-Caribbeans who for the 1991 census gave the Caribbean as their place of birth, at least 83.7% (2,007) were born in Jamaica.[3] It is clear therefore that the dominant African-Caribbean culture and language in Sheffield is Jamaican.

Residence in a black area of Sheffield is one of the variables which influences perceptions of personal identity as well as the vitality of the African-Caribbean community and its language. The areas of Sheffield most densely populated by African-Caribbeans continue to be in the decaying inner city, with poor housing, high levels of unemployment and poverty as well as social problems often associated with newly settled communities (Holmes, 1982: 10, 11). In general, however, the African-Caribbean population of Sheffield is comparatively small and is scattered across many wards of Sheffield.

The African-Caribbean community comprises a number of general social groupings which may overlap or intersect. They include black-led churches, chiefly Pentecostal and Seventh Day, largely in the traditional areas of black population; African-Caribbean community centres which cater for young and old with education and recreation; the Rastafarian community; and young people who belong to none of these organisations but who may 'hang out' in much the same way as the groups Labov (1972) studied in Harlem. Informants for the study were selected from the above social groupings.

It is clear from the above that though the majority of African-Caribbeans have origins in Jamaica the speech community is far from homogeneous. Language loyalties and friendship groups are determined largely by social networks which reflect the organisations to which community members belong. In Sheffield these networks can often be mutually exclusive; interactional networks do not extend to the workplace where contacts with other black people are generally restricted (Edwards, 1986). Some informants, though, do work in a black environment.

The subjects of this research were second- and, in some cases, third-generation Caribbean young people with an identifiable link to one of the local peer group networks discussed above. Collecting data of language use in this community presented logistical problems. Firstly, since Jamaican Creole is regarded as a low-prestige code, which for some of its speakers may not have the status even of a full language as well as an 'insider code' (Milroy, 1987), measures were taken to limit the effect of observer's paradox and to ensure collection of authentic speech data. Labov's (1972) paradigm of the group interview was adopted since it was argued that informants interacting in pre-existing friendship groups, while retaining residual consciousness of the tape recorder, would nonetheless require group members to conform to appropriate linguistic and social behaviour through internal norm-enforcement measures (Labov, 1973; Milroy and Margain, 1978; Milroy, 1987).

Informants formed a judgement sample and were recruited by an intermediary according to pre-determined criteria (Milroy, 1987). These included age, gender, knowledge and use of Creole, willingness to participate in the study and to talk about personal experience of racism and disadvantage at school, in the workplace or in society in general. In addition, and perhaps most importantly, informants were to be recruited as a pre-existing friendship group, since Jamaican Creole operates as an insider code. The original age range of 16–24 had to be extended upwards to accommodate the wider ages often present in friendship groups. The sample was not representative and consisted of nine males and six females.

Based in part on Edwards (1986) a variety of devices were employed in the interviews. These included use of white interviewers for the females to gauge the extent of Creole usage in the presence of out-group members, and use of a black female interviewer to contrast with the male interviewer for the male friendship groups. These devices indicated that African-Caribbean young people interact in Creole more readily and more consistently among the in-group, while for the male friendship groups it was clear they did so to a greater extent in an all-male context.

Background information was collected in formal sequences of the interview, while informal sequences with the presence of an interviewer were included to determine the extent of Creole usage with out-group members. Following Edwards (1986), informants were left alone in the in-group to complete a questionnaire to gauge attitudes to society and towards Creole in general as well as the extent of embeddedness in a local social network. In addition, a brief period of unstructured in-group time was built into the recording sequence which generally preceded completion of the questionnaire. The pretext was preparation of refreshments. It was observed that informants interacted most naturally during this unstructured time and tended to use Creole forms and communication strategies when not otherwise constrained. Interviews were conducted in three different venues according to availability of informants; the researcher's home, an informant's home and a community centre.

Creole usage was analysed quantitatively, to indicate the number of tokens and types of Creole present in the repertoire of informants, as well as qualitatively to establish patterns of interaction. The quantitative analysis was based on two measures: the Creole frequency scale and the Range of Creole Usage Scale (Edwards, 1986).

This measure was based on nine variants (illustrated in Table 10.1) which clearly distinguish Jamaican Creole from English use and which occurred most frequently in the repertoire of informants. The Creole Frequency score was calculated by counting the tokens of Creole and English variants in the vocabulary of informants. This was done by creating word lists and concordances using the Micro OCP computer program (1982) and by checking each instance of Creole usage in the interview transcripts. The number of tokens of Creole and English variants were then totalled for each informant and the following formula used to calculate the proportion of Creole items in relation to overall usage (Edwards, 1986: 79):

$$\frac{\text{No. of tokens of Creole variants}}{\text{No. of tokens of Creole and English variants}} \times 100$$

A score of 100 would indicate completely Creole usage, while a score of 0 would indicate exclusively English usage. Thus speaker (3), who had the highest Creole frequency score of 39.4, registered 1031 Creole tokens and 1587 English tokens. The calculation was as follows:

$$\frac{1031 \text{ Creole tokens}}{2618 \text{ Creole \& English tokens}} \times 100, \text{ i.e.} \frac{1031}{2618} \times 100 = 39.4\%$$

Table 10.1 The linguistic variants in the Creole frequency scale

Variants	Examples of English variants	Examples of Creole variants
1 Dental realisations	/θð/ thin, then	/t d/ / tin, den
2 Vowels /o/ becomes /a/	/o/ knock	/a/ nak
3 Third person sing. present tense verbs (+/- -s)	John swims quickly	Jan swim kwik
4 Plurals	Six cars, all the books	Siks kyaar, aal a di buk (-dem)
5 Simple past tense	Winston saw the boy	Winstan si di bwaay
6 Copulas	The man is happy; the girl is coming	Di man hapi; Di gyal a kom/ komin
7 First person sing. pronoun	I feel happy	Mi fiil hapi
8 Third person sing. pronouns	S/he put it away	(h)im put i(t) wɛh
9 Third person plural pronouns	They like the baby; look at their hats	Dem laik di biebi; Luk pan dem hat

Thus his Creole use represents 39.4% of overall use during the interview. Since Creole language usage in Sheffield occurs in the context of CS it was not anticipated that informants would achieve a score reflecting 100% Creole use.

Gender was the single most important factor influencing the frequency with which informants in this sample used the nine Creole variants in the Creole frequency scale. The male informants used more Creole overall than their female counterparts, the significance level being 0.1%. This correlation may result from the higher level of education among the females in the study and the distance which they might thereby have developed from the vernacular (Labov, 1973). Education did not, however, prove to be a statistically significant influence on Creole frequency (Table 10.2).

The highest scores – with just one exception – are gained by the male informants. Speaker 1, the most highly educated informant, scores lower than female speakers 12 and 10 respectively. This trend would seem to confirm the observation that female speakers are more likely to use standardised forms of language than their male counterparts (Trudgill, 1974).

Table 10.2 The Creole frequency scores

Sex of informant	M	M	M	M	M	M	M	M	F	F	M	F	F	F	F
Record number	3	4	9	8	2	7	5	6	12	10	1	11	14	13	15
Creole frequency score	39.4	37.7	33.5	33.2	29.4	29.2	24.7	23.5	20.2	12.8	12.4	11.1	9.3	6.9	2.9

The range of Creole language scale aimed to indicate Creole grammatical and phonological features in the repertoire of informants. The scale (Table 10.3) consisted of 19 variants, a number of which occurred only with the most proficient speakers. It was thus possible to distinguish between those who used a more limited range of Creole from those with wider application. The score was calculated following Edwards (1986) by counting only the 'types' rather than the tokens of usage. Thus informants needed to register a usage only once for it to be recorded as present in their repertoire.

The count of actual usage by informants detailed below indicates a number of features which typify the speech of all or nearly all speakers irrespective of fluency. These are the dental realisations, the vowels, simple plurals, copulas and pronouns such as yu (possessive second-person plural) and reduction of final consonant clusters. The features which did not occur in the repertoire of a number of speakers were the plural affix '-dem-', the third person plural 'dem', the psychic state transitive verbs, infinitive constructions with 'fi' = 'for', continuatives and Creole question forms (Table 10.4).

Those who have fewest types of Creole usage in their repertoire are the youngest speaker (speaker 7, aged 15) and the most educated (speaker 1). Though the Range of Creole Scores balances out the Creole Frequency Scores, so the difference between male and female informants is marginal, it is nonetheless only the male informants (speakers 2 and 3) who use all 19 of the Creole variants in the scale (Table 10.3).

Realisation of the English dental fricatives [θ] and [δ] by informants was an interesting feature of pronunciation which emerged from the quantitative analysis of language use (Table 10.5). All informants realised these dentals on three levels, the dichotomy between Creole and English dentals – where the majority of tokens occur – and the additional level of realisation, TH-fronting, which falls between the Creole and English and has been termed the Mid-Code. It is possible that the realisation of /δ/ and

Table 10.3 The linguistic variants in the range of Creole usage scale

Variants	Examples of English variants	Examples of Creole variants
1 Dental realisations	/θ ð/ thin, then	/t d/ tin, den
2 Vowels /o/ becomes /a/	/o/ knock	/a/ nak
3 Third person sing. present tense verbs (+/- -s)	John swims quickly	Jan swim kwik
4 Plurals	Six cars, all the books	Siks kyaar, aal a di buk
5 Plurals + 'dem'	the people (plural affix)	di piipl-dem
6 Simple past tense	Winston saw the boy	Winstan si di bwaay
7 Copulas	The man is happy; the girl is coming	Di man hapi; Di gyal a kom/ komin
8 First person sing. pronoun	I feel happy	Mi fiil hapi
9 Third person sing. pronouns	S/he put it away	(h)im put i(t) wɛh
10 Third person plural pronouns	They like the baby; look at their hats	Dem laik di biebi; Luk pan dem hat
11 Other Creole pronouns	2. person plural 2. per. plural possessive	Unu Yu
12 Consonant clusters	Little, ask	Likl, aaks
13 Reduction of final consonant clusters	Must, gift	Mus, gif
14 Glides	Can, boy (to eat)	Kyaan, bwaay, nyam
15 Psychic state transitive verbs	(that)	Tuoni tel mi seh im no nuoh.
16 Infinitives (+fi)	John asked to see it	Jan aaks fi si it
17 Continuatives	The girl is coming	Di gyal a kom/ komin
18 Negatives	The boy does not want it	Di bwaay no waant it
19 Questions	Is Mary going home?	Mieri a go huom?

/θ/ as /v/ and /f/ respectively is a generalised feature of informal regional pronunciation (Trudgill, 1990). In Cockney speech this feature occurs widely (Wells, 1982) and, whereas this replacement may occur in all environments for the voiceless fricative /θ/, e.g. /frIi/ = three; /a:f^{θ}/ =

Table 10.4 The range of Creole usage scores

Speaker no.	Cr. Us. Score	1	2	3	4	5	6	7	8	9	10	11	12	13	14	15	16	17	18	19
1 M	10	✓	✓	—	✓	—	—	✓	✓	✓	✓	✓	—	✓	—	—	—	—	✓	—
2 M	19	✓	✓	✓	✓	✓	✓	✓	✓	✓	✓	✓	✓	✓	✓	✓	✓	✓	✓	✓
3 M	19	✓	✓	✓	✓	✓	✓	✓	✓	✓	✓	✓	✓	✓	✓	✓	✓	✓	✓	✓
4 M	16	✓	✓	✓	✓	✓	✓	✓	✓	✓	✓	—	✓	✓	✓	✓	—	✓	✓	—
5 M	18	✓	✓	✓	✓	✓	✓	✓	✓	✓	✓	✓	✓	✓	✓	✓	—	✓	✓	✓
6 M	15	✓	✓	✓	✓	✓	✓	✓	—	✓	✓	✓	✓	✓	✓	—	—	✓	—	✓
7 M	10	✓	✓	—	—	—	✓	✓	✓	✓	—	✓	—	✓	✓	—	—	—	✓	—
8 M	13	✓	✓	✓	✓	✓	✓	✓	—	—	✓	✓	✓	✓	✓	—	—	—	—	✓
9 M	16	✓	✓	✓	✓	—	✓	✓	✓	✓	✓	✓	✓	✓	✓	✓	✓	—	✓	—
10 F	16	✓	✓	✓	✓	—	✓	✓	✓	✓	✓	✓	✓	✓	✓	✓	—	✓	✓	—
11 F	18	✓	✓	✓	✓	—	✓	✓	✓	✓	✓	✓	✓	✓	✓	✓	✓	✓	✓	✓
12 F	16	✓	✓	✓	✓	—	✓	✓	✓	✓	—	✓	✓	✓	✓	✓	—	✓	✓	✓
13 F	13	✓	✓	✓	✓	✓	✓	✓	✓	✓	—	✓	✓	—	✓	—	—	—	✓	—
14 F	17	✓	✓	✓	✓	—	✓	✓	✓	✓	—	✓	✓	✓	✓	✓	✓	✓	✓	✓
15 F	11	✓	✓	—	✓	—	—	✓	✓	—	—	✓	✓	✓	✓	✓	✓	—	—	—

Table 10.5 TH-Fronting/The realisation of English dental in the speech of informants

Speaker no. >	1	2	3	4	5	6	7	8	9	10	11	12	13	14	15
Creole Frequency Score %age	12.4	29.4	39.4	37.7	24.7	23.5	29.2	33.2	33.5	12.8	11.1	20.2	6.9	9.3	2.9
Creole	104	219	744	342	87	93	36	73	116	101	74	69	39	74	27
English	140	118	88	55	51	93	18	7	20	343	336	139	267	237	352
Mid-Code	95	26	31	41	9	19	11	6	23	6	13	8	6	27	28
Total	334	363	863	438	147	205	65	86	159	450	423	216	312	338	407

Arthur, for its voiced equivalent /ð/ this replacement is only permitted where /ð/ is non-initial. Thus, /faːv/$^\theta$ = father. Contrary to this rule informants were observed in the data to realise /ð/ in the initial position, for example, 'vis' = this, 'vey' = they, 'vi' or 've' = the, 'vere' = there, etc. What is interesting here is whether this aspect of pronunciation is present because it is a Creole innovation (Sutcliffe, 1982), or merely because it is a result of language diffusion having originated in and around London. It is difficult to verify the extent this use is widespead in Sheffield and whether African-Caribbean young people who use it are doing so independently or under the influence of Cockney. Since African-Caribbean young people use the /v/ realisation in environments not documented for other users, it could be argued there is more than one source of influence.

Code-switching Strategies

Conversation analysis (CA) was employed to analyse code-switching (CS) strategies among the sample and to establish the degree of informants' communicative competence in Sheffield Jamaican Creole. Communicative competence in bilingual Creole : English Sheffield is held to comprise shared knowledge of the social significance of various codes of Standard English and regional and informal varieties of English and Creole used in various combinations by informants.

Creole usage in the British context has been represented as the tendency to select forms which are most different from Standard English (Sebba, 1987). However, the data concerning mid-code realisations of English dentals as well as language choice in CS interaction indicate this is not always the case. Alongside the usual types of CS – tag or emblematic switching, intra- and inter-sentential switching – we also note sequences where several turns or utterances are conducted entirely in Creole. Since it is often unclear whether Creole is the matrix or embedded language (Myers-Scotton, 1993), these longer stretches have been labelled 'Creole islands', after Myers-Scotton's 'Matrix- or Embedded-island'. They occur more frequently in the speech of informants who are most prolific in their use and range of Creole forms. Such blocks of Creole speech often coincided with a culture-coded context or were observed as an attention-grabbing device or a means of ensuring a topic change. However, in addition to this pragmatic function, Creole islands demonstrated the competence of speakers in Creole over several turns. In addition, informants also exhibited usages which represent a fusion of the two systems: English syntax with Creole pronunciation and Creole idiom with English pronunciation. These fused or mixed forms of language appear to perform the same function as the mesolect, the mid-point on the Jamaican Creole continuum in the Caribbean context. Indeed, the overlapping and fusion of the two language systems led to the conclusion that, as African-Caribbean young people interact bilingually, they are employing all the linguistic resources available to them in the British situation to define their own identity and their response to the pluralistic environment which surrounds them. Thirteen contexts of CS were also analysed which corresponded to loci of CS represented in the data (Auer, 1995) and transition relevance points where one would anticipate a change of speaker and consequently also CS activity (Mey, 1993) (Tables 10.6 and 10.7).

The most fluent speakers tended to demonstrate a wider variety of types, contexts and tokens of CS and used fewer Creole tokens of types 5 and 6 which reflect a fusion of the two language systems. The females, on the other hand, used more Creole tokens of type 5 and especially of type 6 than their male counterparts which corresponds to their lower scores on the Creole frequency scale. As a result of selecting more fused or mixed forms of language they will have produced fewer distinctively basilectal Creole forms. Are females thereby converging more towards a British identity than males or does their usage reflect a tendency to harmonise two cultural and linguistic identities to a greater degree? (Table 10.8)

CS behaviour has a number of facets and functions as exemplified below. In Example 1, the male informant Speaker 2 is berating his friend for describing Creole as 'Bad English'. His language at this point is characterised by minimal CS (the stereotyped Creole realisation of English 'th') and tags such as 'guy' which has currency as a marker of black identity among older male informants.

Example 1
i   (2)   Ah don't know 'ow you can put dat dahn [that down]. Don't know how you as a Black
ii   man can put dat, guy. 'Bad Inglish'. Should be ashamed of yerself! ... Don't
iii   know 'ow you c'n put da, coz it's not Bad Inglish, at all.

In Example 2, a male informant is expressing his anger and frustration at being ordered around by white superiors at work. This emotion manifests itself in his interaction as intra-sentential switching and quotational switches whereby he quotes the white people in question using Creole, which is certain not to have been the original language they used. This may be a reflection of the strong feelings experienced which, as the data indicate, are often encoded in Creole.

Table 10.6 CS types/tokens realised in the speech data of informants

Speaker no. >	1	2	3	4	5	6	7	8	9	10	11	12	13	14	15
CS type															
1 Tag	19	36	98	31	16	10	17	13	13	24	19	11	9	24	9
2 Intrasent.	86	106	189	166	63	68	27	64	94	96	67	43	45	52	17
3 Intersent.	16	61	166	35	15	19	17	16	48	30	27	51	21	19	10
4 Creole Is	2	24	90	13	10	11	—	1	3	3	6	12	2	8	—
5 Eng/Creole Phon	2	1	4	3	—	1	—	—	—	—	1	1	3	2	4
6 Creole/Eng Phon	3	3	5	4	3	1	2	—	2	11	7	5	8	15	12
Total	138	231	682	252	107	110	63	94	160	164	127	123	88	120	52

Table 10.7 Contexts of CS realised in the speech data of informants

Record No. / CS context	1	2	3	4	5	6	7	8	9	10	11	12	13	14	15
1 Cult	99	111	330	127	49	51	35	63	91	96	63	40	36	73	37
2 Humour	7	17	60	7	6	4	—	2	6	3	6	23	12	2	2
3 Emot. charged	1	39	72	24	13	16	12	3	5	12	4	13	4	16	5
4 Group narr.	19	15	117	12	4	3	—	—	—	7	4	1	6	3	3
5 Quot./ Report. Sp.	4	16	33	15	5	1	4	4	19	19	16	24	23	7	3
6 Adj. Pair	—	7	7	5	1	6	—	1	7	—	—	—	—	2	—
7 Repairs	—	6	9	—	—	—	—	—	—	—	—	—	—	1	—
8 Inserted Sequ.	—	—	3	1	—	—	—	—	1	—	—	—	—	—	—
9 Topic	—	8	13	—	2	—	—	—	2	—	—	2	—	—	—
10 Emph./ Reiterat.	3	9	22	42	21	24	11	19	22	12	7	7	5	6	2
11 Metaling Talk	2	2	12	18	2	5	—	1	5	15	8	9	2	1	—
12 Puns, W-P, Sounding	3	—	4	1	4	—	—	1	—	—	1	3	—	8	—
13 3-Way	—	1	—	—	—	—	1	—	2	—	1	1	—	1	—
Total	138	231	682	252	107	110	63	94	160	164	127	123	88	120	52

Table 10.8 Code-switching tokens of types 5 and 6 by gender of informant

	Context 5 CS tokens	Average score	Context 6 CS tokens	Average score	Total tokens
Male	11	1.22	23	2.55	34
Female	11	1.833	58	9.66	69
Total CS	22		81		103

Example 2
i   (3) (…) yu juss get fed up a dem telling you wat to do, sometimes.
ii (2) [Laugh]
iii (3) 'Du dis, du dat! Du dis, du dat!'
         [Do this, do that! Do this, do that!]
iv MI   (…)
v   (3) 'Go dier, doun't go dier!'
         [Go there, don't go there!]

In Example 3, two of the male informants have a disagreement at the start of the recording session. The informant for whom Creole is a stronger marker of identity (speaker 3) is requiring linguistic and social conformity from his friend. He firstly parodies his friend's previous utterance in Creole (line ii) and then suggests a more socially acceptable manner of expressing his interest (line iii) which is couched in Creole and is dispassionate in nature – perhaps therefore more 'masculine'.

Example 3
i   (1) (…) five minutes … (…)
ii (3) Shaddap! Ee's always dier inní'? 'Af- af- av a nais luk a … pan tings.'
         ['Have- Have to have a nice look at- at things']
iii   Jus seh, 'Bwai, man, ah kud du wid wan a diiz at uom!'
         [Laughter].
         [Just say: 'Boy, man, I could do with one of these at home!']

In Example 4, one of the female informants is seen to use a fused form of English and Creole (line ii – in bold) where the grammar reflects Creole usage though the pronunciation veers towards English phonology.

Example 4
i   (14) Errm .. it was- _mem'- … One time was at SADACCA an' me, Max, an Curtis.

ii   **were drive- They were drivin' mi home. So, Max drivin nice car, bout two**
         [Max was driving a nice car]

iii   a'clock in ve mornin, three a'clock, drivin up my road. Stop up, yu noh.
         [Pulled up, you know!]

In this final example we see evidence of copula deletion or adjectival verbs and omission of the article. It is a narrative on police harassment and illustrates techniques which actualise past events in a manner more in keeping with Creole than with English grammar. Such usages occur when speakers become emotionally involved in their narrative and they can be observed struggling sometimes to express themselves in a culturally relevant manner. Such Creole : English fusions therefore reflect the exploitation of Creole : English language contact to meet the conversational needs of bilingual African-Caribbean young people in Britain.

The contexts in which CS takes place in the data were generally found to correspond to African retentions in Creole languages, reflecting the private, the religious, the culturally different, interacting with aspects of identity in the face of contrary forces. This can be observed in the use of Creole to express 'additional meaning' in contexts defined as 'emotionally charged' such as anger or frustration. In addition, topics or speech which are 'culturally coded' or include details associated with an exclusively black identity, such as family, community or 'back home', tend to trigger CS behaviour as do contexts in which black versus white identity, or 'identity of compromise', are delineated.

It has been demonstrated that language use impinges on identity and identity is interpreted to a degree by the language produced. The females exhibited fewer tokens of Creole and CS in their repertoire and tended to select more mixed forms of language than their male counterparts. This dichotomy corresponds – to some extent – with attitudes towards British society in general. Older males were more critical of society than females and younger males. Their critical attitude coincided with the fact that they had lived in mainly white residential areas with fewer opportunities to engage with black support networks; they would possibly have been more aware of their own out-group status. This may well have been a significant factor for them in defining their identity in terms of language use to release the tension caused by perceived inter-ethnic conflict.

The mix of Creole:English alternation and converging forms which characterised the speech of young African-Caribbeans reflects the bilingual context in which speakers interact. Through language use and combinations of Creole and English, young African-Caribbeans are able to define and redefine their multiple identities, perhaps in defiance of those who do not accord them the status of belonging and who disregard their language as a vehicle of cultural transmission.

Conclusion

The young people in this study demonstrated a knowledge of Creole grammar and were able to perform in Creole, albeit with differing competence. They demonstrated also a knowledge of the rules of bilingual interaction, employing code-switching or code-mixing where the situation required and manipulating the codes at their disposal according to communicative needs and to accepted group norms. The majority of Creole usage took place in the in-group where the widest range of CS types also occurred. Thus the importance of the friendship group as a locus for maintaining and performing in Creole is clearly shown. It is perhaps for this reason, as well as the essentially private and culturally separate nature of CS contexts, that confusion has prevailed concerning the linguistic competence of second-generation Creole speakers.

Informants were observed to use language structures ranging from Standard English or parodies of it, a local, Sheffield variety of English, recreolised English, anglicised Creole to basilectal Creole islands and various combinations of these in their bilingual interaction with in- and some out-group members. There is also evidence of a range of Creole forms in the speech data for all informants in spite of the male:female difference in Creole frequency scores. The latter is partly explained by the propensity among females to use Creole:English fusions (CS types 5 and 6) in greater measure than males, such that their Creole does not always appear as distinct in form from English. In conclusion it is suggested that we see here a redefinition of the Creole continuum to incorporate interaction taking place in Britain. As such, one could also conclude that the redefinition of the Creole continuum highlights the (re)negotiation of identities among young African-Caribbeans in a context where they mean to stay.

Notes
1.   Though the ratio of African-Caribbeans to indigenous population in Sheffield reflects a level above the national average, it is lower than in other centres. For instance, 66.3% of the total Caribbean population of Britain lives in

South-east England, 15.6% in the West Midlands, 4.9% in the East Midlands, 4.3% in Yorkshire and Humberside, but only 1.2% in South Yorkshire (Owen, 1996: 91).
2. Nationally the number of individuals describing themselves in the 1991 census as Black-Other (mixed Black/White) was 24,687, as 'mixed Black/White' 29,882 and as 'Other-Mixed' 61,393. Since many people of mixed parentage are likely to be children of African-Caribbeans the statistics concerning people of African-Caribbean origin is likely to be distorted by the category 'Black-Other'.
3. 1991 Census of Population, Table 7, Country of Birth.

References

Auer, P. (1995) The pragmatics of codeswitching: A sequential approach. In L. Milroy and P. Muysken (eds) *One Speaker, Two Languages: Cross-disciplinary Perspectives on Codeswitching* (pp. 115–35). Cambridge: Cambridge University Press.
Bailey, Beryl L. (1971) Jamaican Creole: Can dialect boundaries be defined' In Dell Hymes (ed.) *Pidginization and Creolization of Languages* (pp. 341–8). Cambridge: Cambridge University Press.
Census 1991 (1992). Office of Population, Censuses & Surveys County Report – South Yorkshire (Parts 1 & 2). London: HMSO.
Edwards, Viv (1986) *Language in a Black Community*. Clevedon: Multilingual Matters.
Gilroy, Paul (1987) *There Ain't No Black in the Union Jack: The Cultural Politics of Race and Nation*. London: Routledge.
Gilroy, Paul (1993) *The Black Atlantic: Modernity and Double Consciousness*. London: Verso.
Hall, R.A. (1966) *Pidgin and Creole Languages*. Ithaca: Cornell University Press.
Holmes, Colin (1982) The Promised Land? Immigration into Britain 1870–1980. In D.A. Coleman (ed.) *Demography of Immigrant and Minority Groups in the United Kingdom: Proceedings of the 8th Annual Symposium of the Eugenics Society*. London 1981. London: Academic Press.
Labov, William (1972) *Sociolinguistic Patterns*. Oxford, Blackwell.
Labov, William (1973) The linguistic consequences of being a lame. *Language in Society* (2), 81–115.
Mackillop, Jane (1980/81) *Ethnic Minorities in Sheffield*. Sheffield Metropolitan District Education Committee.
Mey, Jacob, L. (1993) *Pragmatics: An Introduction*. Oxford: Blackwell Press.
Milroy, L. (1987) *Language and Social Networks* (2nd edition). Oxford: Blackwell.
Milroy, Lesley and Margain, S. (1978) Vernacular language loyalty and social network. *Belfast Working Papers in Language & Linguistics* (3), 1–58.
Myers-Scotton, Carol (1993) *Duelling Languages: Grammatical Structure in Code-Switching*. Oxford: Oxford University Press.
Owen, David (1996) Size, structure and growth of the ethnic minority populations. In D.A. Coleman and J. Salt (eds) *Ethnicity in the 1991 Census. Vol. 1, Demographic Characteristics of the Ethnic Minority Population*. Office for National Statistics. London: HMSO.

Peach, Ceri (1965) West Indian Migration to Britain: The economic factors. *Race* (VII) 1, 31–46.

Peach, Ceri (1968) *West Indian Migration to Britain: A Social Geography*. London: Open University Press.

Peach, Ceri (1982) The growth and distribution of the black population in Britain 1945–1980. In D.A. Coleman (ed.) *Demography of Immigrant and Minority Groups in the United Kingdom: Proceedings of the 8th Annual Symposium of the Eugenics Society*. London 1981. London: Academic Press.

Ramdin, Ron (1987) *The Making of the Black Working Class in Britain*. Aldershot: Gower Publishing Co.

Sebba, Mark (1987) Black English in Britain. In S. Aburdarham (ed.) *Bilingualism and the Bilingual: An Interdisciplinary Approach to Pedagogical and Remedial Issues* (pp. 44-65). Oxford: NFER Nelson.

Sutcliffe, David (1982) *British Black English*. Oxford: Blackwell.

Trudgill, P. (1974) *The Social Differentiation of English in Norwich*. Cambridge: Cambridge University Press.

Trudgill, P. (1990) *The Dialects of England*. Oxford: Blackwell.

Wells, J.C. (1982) *Accents of English. Vol. 2. The British Isles*. Cambridge: Cambridge University Press.

Whyte, Millicent (1977) *A Short History of Education in Jamaica*. London: Hodder and Stoughton.

Chapter 11

Punjabi/Urdu in Sheffield: Language Maintenance and Loss and Development of a Mixed Code

MIKE REYNOLDS

Language shift (LS) is seen as a part of the broader phenomenon of language loss (LL) which, according to de Bot (2001: 66), should be considered as having two aspects: language attrition, the gradual decline over time (e.g. a generation) of language skills, and LS, a process of incomplete transmission and incomplete acquisition of a language. Whereas most investigators have seen LS as a community phenomenon, de Bot sees it from the perspective of the individual speaker. In this study the focus has been on individual families and efforts have been made to involve as representative a sample as possible of the Punjabi community in Sheffield. The focus has also been on individuals' reported and observed behaviour concerning language use, not on language attrition. Given the numbers of participants, it is not valid to make general assumptions for an entire community. Accordingly, language maintenance (LM) has been defined in this study as the continuing use of community languages (CLs); LL of community languages is seen through use of the dominant language (in this case English) in everyday communication.

The study is based on 48 members in 10 families from the Punjabi community in Sheffield. Community members began arriving in Sheffield in the 1950s and come from Jhelum, Rawalpindi and from Mirpur in northeast Pakistan. More than one variety of Punjabi is spoken; however, the majority of community members in Sheffield speak the Mirpuri dialect. The families in the study represent a cross-section (though not a random one) of the community in terms of family structures (e.g. three-generational, extended and nuclear), head of household occupation and area of residence. There are four members of the 'grandparent' (GP) generation two male and two female), 19 of the 'parent' (P) generation (10 male and nine female) and 25 of the 'children' (C) generation, born in the United Kingdom (10 male and 15 female, with 11 under the age of 11 and 14 over). 'Children' was defined as 'being in full-time education'. Eight of the families live in areas of relatively high 'residential contiguity' (Holmes *et al.*, 1993: 15) – one of their conditions favouring language maintenance – and two live in areas where there are few fellow Punjabis. Two of the families are interconnected by having brothers as heads of household, and another three are similarly linked by sibling ties. In all families there are links to family members at a distance, elsewhere in the UK and in Pakistan, the significance of which will be demonstrated.

Underlying the study was the hypothesis that it is possible to make predictions about loss or maintenance of CLs by correlating social network membership with language choice and code-switching behaviours. The social network is a concept well-established in sociolinguistics (e.g. Cheshire, 1978; Milroy, 1987); it was also used by Li Wei and the team studying LM and LL among the Chinese community in Newcastle-upon-Tyne (Li Wei, 1994; Milroy and Li Wei, 1995) which – given their similar concerns – is of relevance to the present study. It is seen as the most valuable concept for linking the macrosociological level of community with the microlevel of interaction which is essential to understand and explain actual sociolinguistic behaviour.

For each family member, interview and observation helped lead to completion of a 'social network profile sheet'. Three types of social network tie were elicited, based on the Newcastle Chinese study (Li Wei, 1994). Firstly there are 'exchange ties' – people with whom one has frequent contact, and to whom one turns for moral and/or material support or advice when in a crisis; typically close family and friends. Secondly there are 'interactive ties' – acquaintances not relied upon for support in a crisis; typically neighbours, shopkeepers, colleagues. Thirdly there are 'passive ties' – typically relatives and friends who live at some distance and whom one does not contact frequently, but on whom one would rely for moral or material support.

The percentages of each type of tie were calculated for each participant on two parameters: the percentages of each type of tie who were Punjabi and/or Urdu speakers (the *ethnic tie percentage score*) and the percentages of those who were of the same age group (the *peer tie percentage score*). The ethnic tie percentages for each participant are given in Table 11.1 in the fourth column.

Exchange ties were found across the generations to be by far the most numerous; interactive ties the least. Children were able to name an average of only five such ties, and parents only six. Exchange ties averaged 25 overall and passive ties averaged eight (nearly ten for the parents, and about seven for each of the children and grandparent generations). Moreover the majority of exchange ties were with close family members rather than friends: nearly 70% for parents and over 80% for grandparents. With the children, the percentage of family exchange ties was not so high but was still in the majority, at an average of 56%. Only a quarter of the children said they spent as much time with friends as with family.[1] In effect the typical Punjabi social network is one of kinship, with the extended family occupying the central position, and non-kin friends seen as less significant.

The social network profiles were analysed by logistic regression to find the significant factors affecting self-reported language choice in terms of age, type of interactant and ethnicity of interactant. From this analysis an implicational scale was drawn up, with a high degree (95.36%) of scalability (see the last six columns in Table 11.1 which show the reported language choices with different types of interactant arranged implicationally). Regression analysis showed age is the significant factor in language choice. The older one is (among family and friends) the greater the likelihood of speaking Punjabi/Urdu.

Although the percentages of exchange ties with fellow Punjabis were generally high to very high,[2] the shared ethnicity is *not* a significant factor except in friend–friend interaction where it is highly significant ($p = 0.002$). This is not surprising given the generally high level of ethnic exchange ties for all participants in the study. Nor is it surprising that it should be significant between friends; this simply shows that the higher the number of Punjabi friends, regardless of age, the more likely one is to speak Punjabi (or Urdu) with them. Although a Pearson product moment test shows a correlation between age and ethnic exchange tie percentages, it is not a strong one ($p = 0.543$); statistically, the two variables remain independent. The implicational scale (Table 11.1) shows two things: the effect of age on the likelihood of choosing a CL rather than English in exchange tie interaction overall; and, by looking across the rows, the likelihood of choosing a CL or English by different types of interactant.

As far as age is concerned, the finding is generally in line with those of the Newcastle Chinese study. The child generation groups towards the top of the table use English either exclusively (4) or predominantly (3) with their peer groups (siblings, cousins and friends). These are *English-dominant bilinguals* and, in one case, a five-year-old girl (#1) an *English monolingual/passive bilingual*. The parent generation is clustered in the middle, using predominantly Punjabi/Urdu (2) with partners, in-laws,

Table 11.1 Implicational scale of language choice (self-reported) by interactant type

	Generation (gender)	Age	Ethnic exchange %	GP	P	PR	S	C	FR
41	C(f)	5	41.66		4		4		4
2	C(f)	16	67.56		2		4		4
23	C(m)	9	70.0		2		4		3*
3	C(m)	13	62.16		3		1*		4
37	C(m)	12	63.88		2		3		4
18	C(f)	17	76.47		1		4		4
6	C(f)	10	50.00	3*	2		3		4
21	C(f)	11	78.78	1	2		4		4
19	C(f)	16	85.71	1	2		4		4
14	C(m)	10	53.85		2		2		4
22	C(m)	10	65.00		2		3		3
33	C(m)	13			2		2		4
12	C(f)	17	33.33		1		3		4
45	C(f)	9	90.90	1	1		4		3*
20	C(f)	14	71.87		2		2		3
17	C(f)	18	66.66		2		2		3
11	C(m)	20		1	2		4		
7	C(f)	4	57.14	1	2		2		4
34	C(m)	7	100.00	1	1		3		4
38	C(f)	9	65.62	1	2		3		3
44	C(m)	11	81.81	1	1		3		4
32	C(f)	18	100.00	1	2		3		3
25	P(f)	23	66.66		1	2		3	3
26	P(f)	28	81.82		1	2	2	3	3
46	C(m)	6	87.50	1	1		3		3
13	C(f)	12	50.00	1	1		3		3
10	C(f)	18	68.75	1	2				3
24	P(m)	24	96.95		2	2		2	2
15	P(m)	44	87.50		1			2	3
1	P(m)	46	79.41				1	2	3
48	GP(m)	61	89.29				1	2	3
39	P(m)	30	100.00		1	2	2	2	2
30	P(m)	41	93.10		1	1	2	2	3
40	P(f)	31	81.81		1	2	2	2	1*

Table 11.1 Continued

	Generation (gender)	Age	Ethnic exchange %	GP	P	PR	S	C	FR
27	P(m)	37	93.75		1	1	1	3	2*
36	P(f)	40	63.63		1	1	2	1*	3
35	P(m)	40	90.48		1	2	2	1*	2
16	P(f)	36	100.00		1			2	2
8	P(m)	47	90.90			1		2	2
9	P(f)	48	96.87			1		2	1*
42	P(m)	34	100.00		1	2	1*	2	1*
4	P(m)	40	58.33			1	1	1	3
43	P(f)	30	100.00		1	1	1	2	1*
5	P(f)	30	100.00			1	1	1	1
31	P(f)	36	100.00		1	1		1	1
29	GP(f)	65	100.00			1		1	1
47	GP(f)	65	100.00					1	1
28	GP(m)	70	100.00			1		1	1

Note:
Asterisk denotes an unscaleable cell, i.e. one that does not conform to the implicational scale.

siblings and their children, Punjabi/Urdu only with *their* parents (the GP generation), and a mixture of predominantly community language (2) or predominantly English (3) with non-kin friends. These are *Punjabi/Urdu dominant bilinguals*. Finally, there is a group of three grandparents and two mothers who stay at home. They report using Punjabi/Urdu with all types of interactant; these are classified as *Punjabi/Urdu monolinguals* (though, noticeably, they all do insertional codeswitching).

Concerning (2), there is a decreasing likelihood of choosing to use a community language as one moves from grandparent to friend. With one (non-scaleable) exception, it is universal to use the community languages to grandparents. With friends the exclusive or predominant use of English prevails among the C and many of the P generations. Husbands and wives use Punjabi/Urdu with each other either exclusively or predominantly. With only two exceptions it is the same with parental interaction. With siblings the pattern is more varied; eight use only English, ten use it predominantly, while five say they predominantly use Punjabi/Urdu. One male teenager says he only uses community languages (this is an unscaleable cell).

In addition to self-report data, the codeswitching (CS) behaviours of the participants were analysed from about 35 hours of recorded talk, mainly in the home. This gave a record of what people do to set alongside what they say they do. The two forms of data were compared by cross-tabulation and the results shown in the graph in Figure 11.3 on page 153.

Codeswitching is typically of two types: 'insertional' and 'alternational' (Muysken, 1995; Guowen Huang and Milroy, 1995). An insertional switch involves insertion of a lexical item or phrase from a donor (or embedded) language (EL) into a matrix language (ML) frame, without any change in the ML frame of the turn. In Example 1, the English lexical item *school* is inserted into a turn with Urdu as ML.

Example 1
(I = male, aged 43)
I: aur kia karte ho *school* mɛ?
[and what do-PAST school-in?]
{and what did you do in school?}

Alternational switching involves a change of languages, and may occur at inter- or intra-clausal levels. Maximally, it involves a change of language with a change of speaker and turn, as in Example 2.

Example 2
(I = father, aged 43; W = son, aged 7)   {Type 1}
I: tell me when to stop alright W ...
(c. 2 seconds)
W: *bohat teez kerte ho na*
{very fast do-PRES. CONT. it, TAG}
[you're doing it very fast, aren't you?]

[IFT/NE/8/T1]

Example 3 is an example of an intra-turn alternational switch at clause level.

Example 3
(R = female, aged 29)   {Type 4}
R: Saba pucho sɔb se, Saba pucho nah.   *Ask the question*
[Saba ask everyone, Saba ask-CAJOLER.]
{Saba, ask everyone, Saba go on, ask.   Ask the question}

[RIF/NE/7/T3: turn 203]

Example 4 is an example at phrase level: it is an 'EL island' (Myers-Scotton, 1993a).

Example 4
    (G = young mother and housewife, aged 24)   {Type 4}
G: X.....X keh k∂rna *around here*?
    [what DO-INF. around here?]
    {[untranscribable] what is there to do around here}
                                                    [ISH/SH/6/T6: turn 37]

The directionality of codeswitching was also taken into account. Alternational switching, involving a switch of ML, could be either from the community languages to English or in the opposite direction. Insertional switching, similarly, could involve English insertion into a CL matrix or vice versa. This gave, overall, four CS types (see Figure 11.1) for counting purposes. In terms of directionality, type 3 is the mirror image of type 2, and type 4 of type 1.

The first point worth noting about CS behaviour is its frequency among nearly all participants and across generations. Percentages of CS occurrence by turns ranges from a high of CS occurrence, of one type or another, in over 70% of that speaker's turns, to below 6%. Parents codeswitched on average in nearly 40% of their turns, children in nearly 35%, and grandparents in about a quarter.

Second, children codeswitch to much the same extent as adults, which contradicts the finding of Farhat Khan (1991), in a study carried out with Urdu speakers in Newham, London. She found that younger speakers (defined as under 30 years old) codeswitched less than older (over 30) speakers. Khan further took this decline in codeswitching in the younger speakers as evidence of language loss. In the present case, given that the

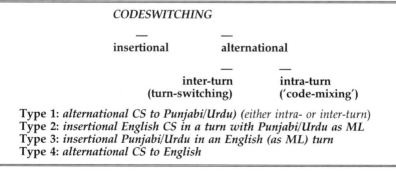

Figure 11.1 Codeswitching types

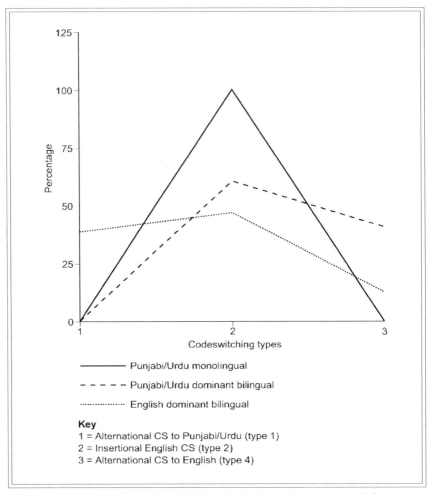

Figure 11.2 Overall codeswitching behaviour by reported language dominance

link between CS and language loss or maintenance can be made, the cross-generational frequency of CS is evidence for CL maintenance.

Parents and grandparents (with one exception) have a clear orientation to the community languages in their switching; that is, they predominantly use type 1 alternational and type 2 insertional switching. What is particularly striking, however, is that also many children (44%) have an orientation to the CLs in their switching and, like their parents, predominantly use type 2 (insertional English) switching (see Figure 11.2).

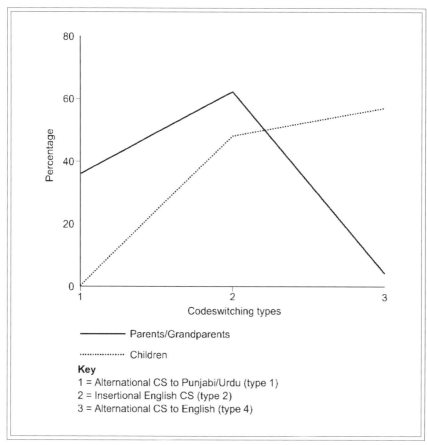

Figure 11.3 Overall codeswitching behaviour by generation

Type 3 switching was the least frequent. It was employed by some of the children, those that could be classified as 'passive bilinguals', and often took the form of 'formulaic' insertions such as use of kinship terms inserted into an English ML turn, as here by H, a four-year-old girl.

Example 5
H: look, look, *Zara bajee, Zara bajee*
        [Zara sister-RESPECT]

[RIF/NE/7/T3: turn 63]

Figure 11.2 also shows how CS behaviours differ between generations. However, type 1 switching by children is almost non-existent, whereas among parents it is the predominant pattern in eight out of 19 cases. On the other hand, type 4 switching (alternational to English) is the predominant pattern for 13 out of the 25 children.

Finally, when CS behaviour across generations is cross-tabulated with reported language dominance (see Figure 11.3) it is seen that Punjabi/Urdu monolinguals (three grandparents and two housebound mothers) use only type 2 switching, but that this is also the predominant pattern, by small majorities, for those who report themselves as bilinguals, whether English or CL dominant. This finding is in contrast to the Newcastle Chinese study. There, similar to the situation among Punjabis in Sheffield, Chinese monolinguals and Chinese-dominant bilinguals used only insertional switching while the English-dominant bilinguals – in the main the younger speakers – were found to prefer alternational switching with both parent and peer generation speakers. The significance of this finding in terms of LM/LL is that in the Newcastle study the assumption was made that rapid shift from the CL was taking place. If the correlation between CS types and LM/LL is valid, then the preference among Punjabi community members in Sheffield for insertional switching would not support a hypothesis of rapid CL loss. However, one conclusion has to be that language loss *is* taking place, but that it is gradual rather than rapid. The main evidence for this comes from the fact that, on the whole, children are talking in English to their peers (friends and siblings and cousins of their own age). On the other hand, parent generation members speak in Punjabi to each other (and often in Urdu to their children) and everyone speaks in Punjabi or Urdu to members of the grandparent generation.

The evidence from the recorded data, however, gives good grounds for believing that Punjabi and Urdu are being maintained at least in the home. Overall any loss is slow and one can point to various factors for this. First and foremost, the CLs are used in the home. This, according to Fishman (1991) and Holmes *et al.* (1993: 16), is the *sine qua non* for LM. Second, social networks with the high number of kinship ties across the generations ensure that contact with the CLs is constant. A third factor is the regularity of contact with Pakistan, giving passive kinship ties, and also for finding marriage partners. This meets two more of the conditions favouring LM outlined by Holmes *et al.* (1993), namely 'a positive orientation to the homeland' and 'resistance to interethnic marriage' (Holmes *et al.*, 1993: 17–19). Finally, evidence from CS behaviours suggests that LM is occurring, both from the fact that younger as well as older speakers codeswitch quantitatively to similar extents and in the same way, namely type 2 insertional.

A third finding, arising from the second, is that a 'mixed code' is developing, and perhaps has been for some time, but its recognition has been obscured by approaches to language contact phenomena that have centred theoretically on a separation of languages to the exclusion of the possibility of fusion of codes in bilingual performance.

Much attention, particularly from an interactional and conversational perspective (Auer, 1998b), has focused recently on the phenomenon of 'mixed code', and it is certainly plausible to see Punjabi and Urdu use in Sheffield involving development of 'mixed code'. In a study of Punjabi in Birmingham in the 1980s Suzanne Romaine (1984) wondered whether the language had achieved 'stable variability'. Findings from the present study, carried out approximately 15 years later, albeit in a different British city, would suggest the answer is in the affirmative. This assertion depends in part on the evidence of development of a 'mixed code', in which elements of English have been embedded into Punjabi and Urdu speech in a regular and predictable manner, as will be outlined below. It is plausible to see this development rising from long contact between English and languages of the Indian sub-continent, notably Hindi, Urdu and Punjabi.

Peter Auer asks whether intra-clausal or intra-turn CS should be regarded as codeswitching at all. The key distinction between CS and mixed code, he claims, has to do with the functionality of the switching, and he has defined 'mixed code' thus (Auer, 1998a: 16):

> Mixed codes contain numerous and frequent cases of alternation between two languages when seen from the linguist's point of view, *but these singular occurrences of alternation do not carry meaning* qua *language choice for the bilingual participants* (although they will usually be able to recognise them). [My emphasis.]

In this view, CS is seen, effectively, as a form of marked discoursal behaviour, and 'mixed code' is more akin to what Myers-Scotton (1993b) has called 'CS as an unmarked choice'.

In our data we found evidence of 'mixed code' at the morpho-syntactic and lexical levels. At the morphological and syntactic level this involves *fusion* or, in Alvarez Cáccamo's words, 'an alloy of two or more speech varieties' (1998: 39), though there is much argument whether the 'fused items' to be described below should be seen as borrowings or as code-switches (Muysken, 1995; Myers-Scotton, 1992; Poplack and Meechan, 1998, and other contributors to the special issue on loanwords and codemixing of the *International Journal of Bilingualism*). Two 'mixed code' processes long noted as a feature of English language contact with Hindi, Urdu and Punjabi (Kachru, 1978; Romaine, 1984, 1989) are *verb compounding* and *noun reduplication*.

Verb compounding is the process whereby an English noun, verb or adjective is combined with a Punjabi or Urdu verbal operator (*kƏrna: to do*, and *hona: to be*), to [[produce a]]

Example 6
{Q = male, aged 13}
Q: *draw keeta* sa *paper* oos na oopƏr Sheffield United
     [draw-DO-PAST 3S MASC. PAST paper that-of Sheffield United]
     {he drew Sheffield United on a piece of paper}
     sign keeta sa   aur sire oopƏr lai sa
     [sign 'DO'-PAST 3S MASC. and head-over put-PAST]
     {signed it and put it over his head}
                                        [AK/BH/1/T2: turn 27]

Example 7
(D = female, aged 17)
D: mε *revise konee keeta*
     [I revise not NEG. -DO-PAST]
     {I haven't revised anything}
                                        [AK/BH/1/T4: turn 129]

Example 8
(W = male, aged 7)
W: *light on* karo
     [light on DO-IMP.]
     {put the light on}
                                        [IFT/NE/8/T1: turn 13]

Example 9
(W = male, aged 28)
W: tussā *check nei score keeta*?
     [you-RESPECT check NEG. score DO-PAST]
     {didn't you check the score?}
                                        [MR/FP/12/T9-B; turn 40]

Noun reduplication is exemplified in Examples 10 and 11, in both of which the ML is Punjabi.

Example 10
(R.B. = female, aged 65)
R.B.: koi *drawer-shrawer* khol na
[any drawer-REDUP. open-REQUEST]
{please; open any drawer}
[IFT/NE/8/T7: turn 36]

Example 11
R.B.: koi *bookā shookā* rakhe hɛ yah zabaaneeh
[any books keep BE-3 PLURAL or memory]
{do you keep/have any books {for assembly} or do you do it from memory?}
[RIF/NE/7/T9: turn 278]

Two other 'mixed code' features that appeared frequently in our data were *Punjabi/Urdu plural affixation on English nouns*, as in *bookā* [books] in Example 11, and here:

Example 12
(S = female, aged 31)
S: *teachrā* ne samNe saariā ni bolti bɔnd hoNi e henh
[teachers-of in front all-PL.-of speech close BE-HABIT. 3S FEM. AUX. 3S]
{faced with teachers, everyone loses their tongue}
[MR/FP/12/T4: turn 62]

and *noun compounding* (English noun + Punjabi or Urdu postposition + English noun):

Example 13
{K = male, aged 34}
K: *school ka work* kia hɛ?
[school-of work what AUX. 3S.
{have you got any school work?}
[MR/FP/12/T4: turn 146]

Example 14
{W = male, aged 7}
W: haā, mɛ yeh (h)or crisp (h)or *do bottles ki milk* (h)or top
[yes, I this or/and crisp or/and two bottles of milk or/and top]
{yes, I had this and crisps and two bottles of milk and (top)}
[RIF/ECC/9/T6: turn 206]

Whereas in Example 13 the word order in the NP is Punjabi/Urdu, so it can be claimed that the CL is the ML at this point. Example 14 is particularly interesting in that the NP conforms to the head first word order of the embedded language and is ungrammatical in Punjabi. This looks like an example of the convergence that Sebba (1998) describes as a defining feature of 'mixed codes'.

A second form of 'mixed code' in Punjabi/Urdu usage in Sheffield is at the level of lexical insertions and depends on the distinction drawn (e.g. by Myers-Scotton, 1992) between 'core' and 'cultural loans'. The evidence for the development of a 'mixed code' comes from the employment of lexical insertions of a 'non-cultural' kind – i.e. where alternatives exist readily in Punjabi and Urdu but where the English lexical item is regularly preferred. Such insertions do not undergo morphological adaptation. Examples of lexical categories of this kind in the data are *numbers, times, days, months, seasons, names of countries, colour words* and *fruits.* The first mentioned, the insertion of English number words into a CL matrix, is claimed by Auer to be evidence for '[the] final step on [the] route towards a mixed code', namely 'the use of language B materials to the exclusion of the equivalent forms in the surrounding language A' (1998b: 17). However, there is considerable variation in the choice of language for number words. This variation can occur even in the same turn at talk, as illustrated here.

Example 15

    (F = male, aged 40)
F: yeh *ten pound* ka tha, yeh aaTh *pound* ka hɛ ab
    [this ten pound-of was, this eight pound-of AUX. 3S PRESENT now]
    {this was ten pounds, now it's eight pounds}
                                                 [RIF/ECC/9/T8-B; p. 19]

English words for the days of the week are the norm. However, there is variation as the following example shows. One speaker uses the Urdu word for Monday, whilst her interlocutor uses the English form for Tuesday.

Example 16

    (S = female, aged 31; Sh = female, aged 30)
25   S: *Tuesday* ko (keh raha hɛ) afternoon
           [Tuesday-on say-CONT.3S MASC. AUX. afternoon]
           {He's saying that (it)'s on Tuesday afternoon}

26   Sh: aap ko kaha tha   Somwaar ki r∂khe Pir ke din subah
             [you-FORMAL-to say-PAST Monday-to arrange Monday -on
             day morning]
             {I told you to arrange it on Monday, on Monday morning}
27   S: nahi mε aa jaaya karoō g *Tuesday afternoon*
             [NEG. I come-from-home -DO +FUT. 3S. FEM.]
             {No, I can come on Tuesday afternoon}
                                        [MR/FP/12/T5: turns 25–27]

    The next example illustrates use of English to refer to fruit, although it
is possible that with this category the insertions may be 'cultural loans'
rather than evidence of 'mixed code'. Fruits commonly consumed in this
country, such as oranges and pears, may be associated more with this
country than with Pakistan, and so have entered into bilingual discourse
as loans rather than as codeswitches.

Example 17
             (As = male, aged 40; K = female, aged 30; F = female, aged 4)
      As: kehRa hisaab kitaab kh∂Rnās?
             [what else take-FUT. 3S]
             {what else will she take?}
K:→   *pear*
F:→   *pear* hunh   [AK/BH /2/T9: turns 48–50]

    There is more work to be done on the development of mixed code, in
particular among the Punjabi/Urdu speaking community in Sheffield and
in general in the UK. For instance, what are the circumstances that
encourage 'mixed code'? Does a 'mixed code' develop in all situations of
prolonged language contact or only in some? Is frequency of CS – a
feature of the Punjabi community – one of the conditions favouring
mixed code development? What forms does 'mixed code' take? 'Core'
lexical insertions as outlined above would appear to be one manifestation. Auer (1998b) and Maschler (1998) have suggested that discourse
markers are another. Sebba (1998) describes a number of strategies of
'convergence'. One of these, the *neutralisation strategy* (Sebba, 1998: 11–
12), can be seen in verb-compounding described above and this suggests
fruitful directions for the investigation of 'mixed code'. Above all, looking
at CS, where it is the interactional norm of bilingual discourse, as the
possible development of a 'mixed code' which cannot be described in
terms of monolingual grammars, allows us to break from the
monolingual bias presupposed in the very notion of code-*switching* and

adopt what Meeuwis and Blommaert (1998) have dubbed the 'monolectal view of code-switching'. From this perspective CS is not regarded as 'marked' speech – though it *may* of course be used for such a purpose, as is the case in CS *between the two CLs* in those families with a policy of speaking Urdu rather than Punjabi to the children. An example of this familial 'language policy' at work is shown in Example 18, where the parent (F) switches from speaking Punjabi to a fellow adult to address his child (S) in Urdu:

Example 18

(S = daughter (aged 4); F = S's father (aged 40), Ha = F's brother (aged 40+))

19 S: x you come here
20 F: {U} a**ch**a abhi aate hɛ
 [fine now come-FUT. BE-1PL.]
 {OK, we'll come now}
21 Ha: {U} **wo aapne baDi x aate hɛ**
 [that you-RESP. NOM. big ? come-FUT. 3PL./RESP.]
 {you've done that well; he'll come}
22 F: {P} *x jitna marzi chahida akhia*
 [? as much desire want-3S say-PAST PART.]
 {he said as much as he wanted to}
 [RIF/ECC/9/T8-A: turns 19–22]

In the specific case of Punjabi/Urdu-English bilingual discourse, work has still to be completed on the following areas: the ratio of 'fused forms' to other type 2 insertions; the frequency of 'core' lexical insertions compared with 'cultural' insertions, and finally, the generative productivity of verb compounds, where there is a range from the simple noun, or verb plus verbal operator (as in Example 6) to the more complex phrasal structure with negation, as in Example 10.

Finally, one can ask whether 'mixed code' is evidence of CL maintenance or loss. Here the answer will depend on how stable mixed code is. As already noted, some at least of the processes of 'fusion' in Urdu and Hindi-English contact have been attested for a long time. This by itself would suggest that mixed code is evidence for language maintenance, insofar as it is evidence of language contact which is accepted and established, and in which members of a close-knit kinship network feel comfortable. In the home CS is frequently the 'unmarked code' (Myers-Scotton, 1993b), and the use of 'mixed code' is reminiscent of what Swigart in his study of Urban Wolof in Dakar (Swigart, 1992) claims is an established variety (although he claims further that it is growing in use *and* number of domains). The conclusion, then, is that in the case of Punjabi/Urdu in Sheffield 'mixed code' is evidence more for language maintenance than for loss.

Notes

1. The ranges by generation were: 100–90.7% for grandparents, 100–57.6% for parents and 90.9%–33.3% for children. One-way ANOVA showed that generation affected ethnic exchange ties percentages in a highly significant manner (F, 11.61, $p = 0.000$). This significance was confirmed by a Kruskal-Wallis test which does not assume a normal distribution of the ethnic exchange ties.
2. A two-sample t-test showed that the difference in mean percentages of CS by children and parents was not significant ($p = 0.25$). Grandparents were excluded from this test as their numbers were too small – four – for results to be statistically valid.

References

Alladina, S. and Edwards, V. (1991) *Multilingualism in the British Isles. Vol. 2.* London: Longman.

Alvarez Cáccamo, C. (1998) From 'switching code' to 'code-switching'. In P. Auer (ed.) *Code-switching in Conversation: Language, Interaction and Identity* (pp. 29–48). London: Routledge.

Auer, P. (1995) The pragmatics of code-switching: A sequential approach. In L. Milroy and P. Muysken (eds) *One Speaker, Two Languages* (pp. 115–35). Cambridge: Cambridge University Press.

Auer, P. (ed.) (1998a) *Code-switching in Conversation: Language, Interaction and Identity.* London: Routledge.

Auer, P. (1998b) Introduction: *Bilingual Conversation* revisited. In P. Auer (ed.) *Code-switching in Conversation: Language, Interaction and Identity.* (pp. 1–24). London: Routledge.

Cheshire, J. (1978) Present tense verbs in reading English. In P. Trudgill (ed.) *Sociolinguistic Patterns in British English.* London: Edward Arnold.

de Bot, Kees (2001) Language use as an interface between sociolinguistic and psycholinguistic processes in language attrition and language shift. In Jetske Klatter-Folmer and Piet van Avermaet (eds) *Theories on Maintenance and Loss of Minority Languages: Towards a More Integrated Explanatory Framework* (pp. 65–81). Muenster: Waxmann.

Eastman, C. (ed.) (1992) Codeswitching. *Journal of Multilingual and Multicultural Development* 13, 1 & 2.

Fishman, Joshua A. (1991) *Reversing Language Shift: Theoretical and Empirical Foundations of Assistance to Threatened Languages.* Clevedon: Multilingual Matters.

Guowen, H. and Milroy, L. (1995) Language preference and structures of code-switching. In D. Graddol and S. Thomas (eds) *Language in a Changing Europe* (pp. 35–46). Clevedon: BAAL/Multilingual Matters.

Holmes, J., Roberts, M., Verivakim, M. and Aipolo, A. (1993) Language maintenance and shift in three New Zealand speech communities. *Applied Linguistics* 14/1, 1–24.

Kachru, B. (1978) Toward structuring code-mixing: An Indian perspective. *International Journal of the Sociology of Language* 16, 27–47.

Khan, F. (1991) The Urdu speech community. In S. Alladina and V. Edwards (eds) *Multilingualism in the British Isles. Vol. 2* (pp. 128–40). London: Longman.

Li, W. (1994) *Three Generations, Two Languages, One Family: Language Choice and Language Shift in a Chinese Community in Britain.* Clevedon/Philadelphia/Adelaide: Multilingual Matters.

Maschler, Y. (1998) On the transition from code-switching to a mixed code. In P. Auer (ed.) *Code-switching in Conversation: Language, Interaction and Identity.* (pp. 125–49). London: Routledge.

Meeuwis, M. and Blommaert, J. (1998) A monolectal view of code-switching: Layered code-switching among Zairians in Belgium. In P. Auer (ed.) *Code-switching in Conversation: Language, Interaction and Identity* (pp. 76–98). London: Routledge.

Milroy, L. (1987) *Language and Social Networks* (2nd edition). Oxford: Blackwell.

Milroy, L. and Li, W. (1995) A social network approach to code-switching: The example of a bilingual community in Britain. In L. Milroy and P. Muysken (eds) *One Speaker, Two Languages* (pp. 136–57). Cambridge: Cambridge University Press.

Muysken, P. (1995) Code-switching and grammatical theory. In L. Milroy and P. Muysken (eds) *One Speaker, Two Languages.* Cambridge: Cambridge University Press.

Myers-Scotton, C. (1992) Comparing codeswitching and borrowing. In C. Eastman (ed.) Codeswitching. *Journal of Multilingual and Multicultural Development* 13, 19–39.

Myers-Scotton, C. (1993a) *Duelling Languages: Grammatical Structure in Code-switching.* Oxford: Clarendon Press.

Myers-Scotton, C. (1993b) *Social Motivations for Codeswitching: Evidence from Africa.* Oxford: Oxford University Press.

Poplack, S. and Meechan, M. (eds) (1998) *International Journal of Bilingualism* 2(2): Special issue: Instant Loans, Easy Conditions: the Productivity of Bilingual Borrowing.

Romaine, S. (1984) Language loss and maintenance in a multiethnic community, End-of-Grant Report HR8480, Economic and Research Council (ERSC).

Romaine, S. (1989) *Bilingualism.* Oxford: Blackwell.

Sebba, M. (1998) A congruence approach to the syntax of codeswitching. *The International Journal of Bilingualism* 2(1), 1–19.

Swigart, L. (1992) Two codes or one? The insiders' view and the description of codeswitching in Dakar. In C. Eastman (ed.) Codeswitching. *Journal of Multilingual and Multicultural Development* 13, 83–102.